Creativity
Works

BMP **DDB**

Creativity
Works

Edited by
Anneke Elwes

P

PROFILE BOOKS

First published in Great Britain in 2000 by
Profile Books Ltd
58A Hatton Garden
London ECIN 8LX
www.profilebooks.co.uk

and
BMP DDB Ltd
12 Bishops Bridge Road
London W2 6AA
www.bmpddb.com

Typeset in Columbus by MacGuru
info@macguru.org.uk

Printed and bound in Great Britain by
St Edmundsbury Press, Bury St Edmunds

A CIP catalogue record for this book is available from the British Library.

ISBN 1 86197 279 2

Contents

Preface

This book could be subtitled 'Insights into Inspiration'. Its contributors have all succeeded in stimulating organisations and individuals to higher levels of achievement through their leadership and ideas. They have all done inspiring things. So, when asked about the role and nature of creativity in their work, it is not surprising that they have given us a stream of fresh insights about creating change, innovation and new thinking in business and society.

Our interviewees are an eclectic group – corporate leaders, architects, entrepreneurs, academics – but they are united by two characteristics: notable achievement and what we felt was a record of creativity in their field. We have let them tell us what that means to them in their own words, so that a range of perspectives on creativity emerges. Common themes also emerge, which are analysed in the Introduction by Anneke Elwes, our interviewer and editor. One theme is universal: unleashing and encouraging the creativity of individuals, especially when they work together, is like discovering a powerful new lever. It can move mountains.

Of course, creativity is the principal business of those of

us who work in advertising, so agencies have, over the years, evolved working environments that nurture creativity. Interestingly, many of the policies advocated by our interviewees – all of them people whose achievements were accomplished outside advertising – are those found in agencies. Small, non-hierarchical teams, a multi-disciplinary approach, freedom to fail and freedom from fear, a highly competitive environment with high levels of praise and recognition, hunger, energy, fast-tracking for stars – all these aspects of a creative, innovative business habitat that our interviewees challenged their own organisations to adopt and value, are fundamental to good agency practice.

The momentum for this book came from the belief that, in a sense, Britain's strength in the 'creative industries' like advertising has also become a weakness. 'Creativity' can all too easily be seen as the preserve of 'creative' firms and limited to acts of invention. In reality, commercial success depends on creativity throughout a firm's activity, in fresh thinking and inventiveness in people management, marketing, production, selling, finance and all the disciplines of business.

Having just been named the world's most creative advertising agency, we at BMP DDB wanted to discover how some of the UK's most original and successful minds in other walks of life nurtured creativity. We are very grateful to them all for their time and thoughtfulness in sharing their views. Their combined experience echoes Bill Bernbach, one of the founders of DDB and the pioneer of advertising's 'Creative Revolution', who wrote: 'Is creativity some obscure, esoteric art form? Not on your life. It's the most practical thing the businessman can employ.'

James Best, *Group Chairman, BMP DDB Group*
Chris Powell, *Chairman, BMP DDB*

Foreword

I welcome this book. The future of the global economy depends on business creativity – that is, the imaginative application of new solutions to new and to old problems. And Britain's success as one of the world's leading economies depends on creativity more than most. It is probably a myth to imagine that it was ever enough for a company to start up, start making something (widgets perhaps), sell them and then carry on doing so as they had always done. If that world ever existed it has been gone for many years now. Businesses can only survive, prosper and grow in a voraciously competitive global economy if they continually innovate. And innovation means being creative. It means finding new solutions to old problems – either by encouraging people to work in different ways, or through the use of new technology and new processes. It also means finding entirely new products, new routes to market and new markets altogether. Of course creativity is not confined to any one sector of the economy. It is essential in business today. It is also essential in the public sector, arts and, yes, government.

We in Britain are better placed than perhaps we think to lead in the business creativity that will matter in the future.

Because these islands have been open and outward looking this country has fostered not only a vigorously adaptable society but this has given rise to a tolerance and belief in liberty and fair play, and a creativity and inventiveness which is of most direct application to business and our economic future.

From the first agricultural revolution of Jethro Tull and the 'improving farmers' to the Industrial Revolution originated in Ironbridge, Manchester and the great industrial heartlands it continues unbroken to the present day. The current 'post-industrial' economy has its origins in the pioneering work of Charles Babbage, Alan Turing and many others. It extends to many other fields of endeavour too. Inventiveness has ranged everywhere from engineering, the arts and medicine, to the shop floor.

The gap – as has been commented on so many times – is between the creativity on the one hand and the implementation on the other. Too often in the past British genius has created world-changing ideas but the economic opportunities to exploit those ideas have been seized upon and exploited elsewhere. The computer and the Internet are only two of the most recent examples. The ideas and the presiding genius were British. Exploitation (so far, anyway) has been elsewhere. That is what we have to change: we have to learn to adapt and encourage that creativity and make sure that it is implemented and exploited here. We must ensure that this country reaps the benefits of its creativity. In the chapters that follow 20 people talk about ways in which that has been achieved. There are lessons that we can all learn from here.

The role of the government must be to both encourage that creativity and inventiveness, and then to help foster implementation. This means making Britain an attractive place for people to work and for businesses of all scales. We are helping large businesses to expand their markets internationally and we are encouraging new start-ups and entrepreneurs. Interestingly, more inward investment is coming into Britain than any other country in Europe, which shows that people worldwide recognise the changes that are taking place and the opportunities that are opening up.

Creativity is going to be of increasing importance in the twenty-first century when raw materials can be bought from anywhere at any time and economic prosperity and business success depend on ideas, skill and offering what is distinctive, special and original. Those are the qualities that will differentiate Britain from the rest of the world. We are setting out to create an economic environment in which innovation and creativity can flourish and be encouraged. That is why business start-ups are now at an all-time high. That is why there is such excitement in this country about new dot.coms and new entrepreneurs. When I go round the country now I am struck by the fact that when leaving university the brightest and the best no longer head straight for safe professions like banking or the civil service. They are setting up new companies of their own or seeking to soar in some of our world famous companies.

As Chancellor I know that we have to provide a platform of stability for business to invest, provide the right economic environment and encourage people to take risks. Those interviewed for this book reveal a great optimism about what we are capable of achieving and a great awareness of how crucial a role creativity plays in business. We should all be confident of the growing opportunities for real creativity in this country. It is going to shape the Britain of the future.

Gordon Brown, *MP, Chancellor of the Exchequer*

Creativity
Works

Introduction by Anneke Elwes

The way creativity works in business is much talked about but hard to pin down. It is too loose and slippery to be easily measured by scientific analysis or modelled by business theory, and yet something of its richness and complexity does emerge from observing it. The people interviewed for this book approached this many-sided subject from the single starting point of their professional experience. They ascribe to creativity the behaviour and functions that they believe to be the most important in business. It is these insights that expose the less obvious factors that contribute to business success and so reveal the beliefs and passions that inspire great achievement in organisations.

Marrying the term 'creative' to business runs counter to the trend which, over the past decades, has tried to turn business into an applied science with its own theory and language. In the eyes of those outside the corporate world, 'business' appears to have a life of its own, involving a set of rules and performance criteria which set it sharply apart from the cultural conditions and personal qualities that matter to us as individuals. Creativity, on the other hand, is a general condition of humanity. It is often perceived as an individual gift and usually associated with an individual act. Looking at business through the prism of creativity has a strange effect. It both demystifies and humanises business. It also breaks down some of the linear thinking that in the past has not only kept art and culture separate from commerce, but even suggested that they might be antithetical.

The limits of labels

To explore business creativity we need to prevent it from being appropriated by particular sections of business or functions within it. Terms such as 'creative industry' and 'creative director' tend to ghettoise creativity by suggesting that somehow, by virtue of simply applying the word, the world will acknowledge that such industries or people behave more creatively than their 'non-creative' counterparts. This is born of the same set of assumptions which at school decrees that only when you are in the art room are you being creative, and which later on, in business, implies that if you are a 'suit' you are not creative.

The notion that some commercial activities are, by their nature, more creative than others, stems from a belief that creativity is an individual act. So on the one hand you have 'a creative' – or creative team/department – and on the other, those who enable or depend on their creativity. The assumption is that as soon as you have 'creatives' working together, it becomes very hard to organise. Creativity of this nature is not necessarily diminished by numbers, but numbers can militate against its free play. A collaborative act seems somehow intrinsically less creative than an individual one. As someone pointed out, even John Lennon and Paul McCartney mostly worked alone on their songs.

The late 1980s and early 1990s witnessed a huge burgeoning of the 'creative industries', by which was meant industries whose product was perceived, to a great extent, to be the result of individual creativity (i.e. film, advertising, design, fashion, music). 'Cool Britannia' celebrated this tendency in a very public way. As Christopher Frayling says, it helped legit-imise and provide support for activities which had been seen as somewhat marginal to our commercial output. But one danger in celebrating, say, fashion and film over retail and pharmaceu-ticals is that it risks maintaining a picture of British creativity as being maverick and individualist and therefore more difficult to associate with industries that require a disciplined, collaborative approach. It suggests flamboyance without focus, chaos without control. Thus creativity slides into cliché.

The creative potential

Recognising the importance of creativity in all kinds of indus-tries and all kinds of roles within those industries is especially pertinent in the fast-moving business environment of today. What those interviewed for this book reveal is a concern less with one-off flashes of brilliance than with the ability to capture and hold on to a market. Above all, they share a belief about the need to sustain creativity in order to remain consis-tently successful. No mean feat, especially at a time of rapid change when competitive advantage requires anticipating, even inventing, the future. Creativity in this context involves vision, ambition and challenge. It is driven by wanting to be the best and not being satisfied with second best. This compulsive quality may be less explicit when contained in the artist's mind, but it is precisely the same quality that drives the process of cre-ating great works of art. In business as in art the test will be whether the result is successful.

What will become clear to readers of this book is that the qualities we admire in creative individuals are there by the bucket load. But instead of being internalised, they need to be shared in order to empower others and provide the impetus that can carry a business forward. Inspiration may come from within but it is of greatest value when it is shared. In this way it becomes infectious.

The language effect

Our use of language is one of the reasons why creativity sometimes appears to sit uncomfortably with business. Before the word 'business' came to be associated with full-blooded commercial enterprise in the late 19th century, it just meant being 'busily engaged in something' with all its overtones of earnest, diligent labour. The word 'corporation' is not much better with its dull, legalistic overtones and its derivation from *corpus,* or body, suggestive of corpulence. It is not until we use words like 'enterprise' (meaning 'bold undertaking, daring spirit'), 'entrepreneur' (which came to mean 'one who gets up entertainment' in France) and 'innovation' (meaning 'introduce novelties, renew') that excitement begins to creep in. These words have a dynamism that fits more easily with the idea of applying creativity to change and growth.

Connecting is crucial

Often creativity is linked to invention – creating something new. Once the prerogative of the individual, it has tended to become located in business either in the R&D lab or in the new product development department. However, among those interviewed for this book there was strong resistance to the idea that creativity might be the prerogative of one particular function within business. This was because the creativity talked about was more often than not applied creativity – creative thinking that allowed new connections to be made between existing elements. So rather than a pipeline approach – where you pour money into research at one end and commercial applications pop out at the other end – what was more generally favoured was a springboard approach which starts with ideas and insights about the market opportunity. Most of these new ideas are generated through constant dialogue with customers and suppliers – whether it was lastminute.com talking to ticket agencies, Tesco talking to shoppers or Daniel Libeskind talking to cleaners at the V&A. This focus on, and accountability to, stakeholders and ultimately end users, seems to have become far more widespread. It is now the responsibility of everyone, and not simply the marketing department.

The difference these insights can make to a business may be incremental or radical, depending on how creative the response is. The most creative companies see themselves as agents of change, setting out to create tomorrow's markets. In asking the question what to do next, they realise that the answer is not out there, however deep they dig. The creative imperative to challenge existing perceptions, to find new ways to engage with customers and to do things differently from competitors puts great store by listening and observing. Having this degree of sensitivity requires being close to your staff, customers and suppliers so that you can actually observe the process of change. And if the response to what is observed is to be innovative, it requires creative learning. Several contributors – Chris Evans, Dennis Stevenson and Charles Dunstone in particular – spoke about the insights and ideas that had made a big difference as being based on 'instinct', 'seeing what's under your nose' or 'common sense'. But this rather underplays the fact that you need to be well attuned to change in the first place and able to look at the world around you with a wide-angle lens. If it is not what anyone else is doing or thinking at the time, it only becomes obvious with hindsight.

Never give up

Another individualistic quality, singled out by Martha Lane Fox and Gerry Robinson, was doggedness – particularly in the face of doubters. Sheer bloody-mindedness is a characteristic that one does associate with the creative temperament. A tenacious person will find a way to solve a seemingly intractable problem and derive pleasure from proving others wrong. Furthermore, a refusal to abandon a pet idea can allow that person the time needed to find a creative application and re-present it in a new context. As Roger Cairns points out, this was the case with radar – good ideas sometimes need to wait for their moment to arrive. In advertising it used to be called 'the bottom drawer' syndrome and sometimes it provided the genesis of a great new campaign.

Once a problem has been identified you need to work to a solution. The solution may not be quite what you expected but creativity takes many forms. The route is in all likelihood going to be tangential rather than linear as, along the way, it involves learning from mistakes and capitalising on unexpected successes. As Gerry Robinson observes, there's no mechanism for getting at creativity, you cannot really prescribe how things should happen; you enable them to happen.

Getting the culture right

All of which brings us to the cultural conditions for creativity. Cultures can encourage ideas and radicalism; but equally they can discourage them. Companies can, sometimes, be too proud of their own competence and achievements to take note of interesting new ways of doing things happening elsewhere – what has been termed a company's *sense of sovereignty*. Insularity can be born of arrogance. And yet if creativity is the engine for growth and applied creativity is about making new connections, it follows that the more a company is prepared to move out beyond its own four walls, through allegiances, networks and collaborations, the more likely it is to be creative. Helen Alexander noted that the best ideas come from bits of other people's good ideas. Once a creative idea has been conceived it needs others to shape it and give it articulation. Daniel Libeskind suggested that underestimating the contribution that others can make is a failure of vision.

This openness to other people's ideas was a constantly recurring theme in the interviews, particularly from those business leaders with a strong record of sustained success within their sector. Terry Leahy described the management style at Tesco as 'ask more than tell' and spoke of the importance of an open, listening style to nurturing innovation. Brian Pitman and Charles Dunstone echoed this when they emphasised the need to really listen to the organisation and create a culture where ideas can flood in. Gerry Robinson took this one stage further when he spoke of his belief in changing roles for people once they'd proved themselves, to enable them to make new connections by applying their experiences from one area to another. Interesting things can occur when disciplines are encouraged to overlap as Patricia Hewitt witnessed at Textile Jersey. In a company growing as rapidly as lastminute.com this happens through necessity rather than design and yet can result in great breadth of creative experience.

The management challenge

Creativity in the workplace, it was agreed, is essentially about managing human relationships and drawing out the creativity of those around you to commercial effect. There appears to be a sea-change underway in relationships at work. Expectations have changed and the business environment has changed; hierarchical, command-and-control structures and paternalistic attitudes have clearly had their day. Whilst new technology businesses are undoubtedly helping to drive this change with their youth cultures, cellular structures and share options, it is interesting to note Philip Dowson describing that this was exactly this environment at Ove Arup in the 1960s. What was clearly a pioneering approach then has achieved acceptability now. Technology is forcing a reassessment of the kind of work relationships needed to be creative. The new industries which are not held back by the status quo are tackling this with great energy and imagination, whilst many older industries are also reinventing themselves to move forward. This creative regeneration is taking place in some surprising quarters.

Lloyds TSB has made flexible working – accommodating when and where people want to work, regardless of rank – a mainstream business practice. Large corporations are moving from fixed salaries to variable pay with high rewards. John Sunderland tells us that Cadbury Schweppes is providing seed corn funds to help capitalise its own people. In order to keep talent in house, forward thinking companies are attempting to embrace a more entrepreneurial culture that rewards risk taking. With the enthusiastic uptake of share options in early stage companies and the creation of corporate venturing arms, the divide between 'corporate business', with all it implies, and 'enterprise' may begin to narrow.

Size and youth in the creative equation

One of the recurring points of discussion was whether small, young companies are intrinsically more creative than large ones. Undoubtedly the creative challenges continue as a business gets bigger and require the sort of creative response that Martha Lane Fox describes when discussing the growing maturity of last-minute.com. But by and large it was felt that the smaller the company the greater its capacity for risk taking. Young companies are closer to the point of failure than old ones and this makes them more challenging, more flexible and, as a consequence, potentially more creative. Personal responsibility can also result in bold creative moves. As organisations grow bigger they can lose that sense of ownership – the feeling that everyone is in this together and that they care deeply about what happens. A strong sense of ownership can create a more powerful need to find ways to make things work. The more personal an endeavour the more important it is to prove that it can be done.

Risk and reward

Share options, used not as a substitute but as an addition to a good salary, can sustain this sense of belonging. They can also reward risk and increase commitment. And a creative, innovative business has to take risks. Terry Leahy points out that in order to innovate and continue to lead the grocery retail market, Tesco has to operate at a higher level of risk than its competitors. This means accepting that mistakes will be made. Experimenting and trying out new ideas means being prepared to fail.

Entrepreneurs often operate at a very high level of individual risk, as the careers of both Chris Evans and Ian Livingstone pay testament. Homes can be re-mortgaged in order to give it a go. But when the houses are repossessed and the bailiffs turn up, instead of rising from the ashes, many of these would-be entrepreneurs sink without trace. Unlike in the United States, where business failure is accepted as the risk of having a go, there is an expectation in Britain that you should get it right first time. Better bankruptcy laws would undoubtedly help people to learn from their mistakes and try again, but so would a more general acceptance in business that learning is incremental and that repeated attempts can lead eventually to success.

Teaching elephants the creative dance

Large corporate cultures are inclined to become highly judgmental, a factor that can inhibit the most inquisitive and creative learners. Several contributors stressed the importance of dealing creatively with mistakes, since trying something new would more likely be discouraged in a culture of blame and penalisation. An organisation that is not making mistakes is likely to be standing still.

A creative company was described as having a certain edge to it. It needs to be alert to ensure the culture doesn't become lazy. It needs to be vigilant to ensure it maintains a creative range of people. It also needs to be highly ambitious. 'Think big' was the mantra offered by those involved with start-ups and early stage companies. In large corporations too, the practice of setting very high targets and almost unattainable objectives was generally believed to lift expectations and increase achievement. Stretching people encourages them to dig deeper for creative solutions; the challenge brings new ideas to the surface. For organisations with large workforces it was particularly important to have mechanisms in place that would allow management to tap into, and engage with, the combined creativity of the workforce and not just with the creative skills of the odd individual.

Getting the balance right in a large organisation is clearly difficult. The culture needs to empower creativity but it must provide a bedrock of belonging and security. George Orwell noted this when he remarked: *'the tendency is to make our environment safe and soft: and yet you are striving to keep yourself both brave and hard'.*

Contributors agreed that politics, status, fear, hierarchy, and bureaucracy were antithetical to creativity, but on security, control and order there was less consensus. There is no good reason why creativity should not flourish within a disciplined, efficient environment.

Interestingly it was the entrepreneurs, not the professional managers, who felt most comfortable with the 'creative' label. The professional managers would probably not call themselves creative and yet managing others to draw out their creativity is clearly a skill, and probably an under-recognised one. Factors that can create a spirit of enterprise within a larger organisation include the creation of small business units with greater autonomy and freedom from organisational interference. Michael Perry stressed Unilever's adherence to the belief that whilst objectives may be set, how they were to be achieved must never be prescribed. Clearly organisations should not be over managed, if they are to provide the scope and space to allow others to make things happen in their own way.

There was evidence in the conversations of a recognition that, in corporate life, people want to feel that they can grow, balance their life, make an impact and get noticed. Creative organisations understand that they need to accommodate these aspirations to get the best out of people. A great deal of creative emphasis was placed on re-thinking old ways and exploring new ways of employing and incentivising people internally. In addition it was recognised that having a reputation for delivering innovation and being a leader externally had a very powerful motivational effect and could also attract creative people to a company.

Leading the way

Brave, confident leadership that can carry others to greater heights than they may have reached alone was clearly an important catalyst. A good leader's role was to inspire and challenge. In an organisational context, creativity and challenge were often used synonymously: challenging the prevailing thinking, challenging the status quo and challenging employee comfort zones; giving individuals new challenges by taking them out of the familiar and putting them into the unfamiliar. There was an assumption that, unless constantly challenged, organisations would become sleepy and start to put on weight around the waist. It was the Chief Executive's role to maintain vigilance and shake things up at the first sign of the rot setting in. Resistance was anticipated because, again, the assumption was that people, particularly those who join large corporations, don't like change. So, on the one hand there was a need to provide sufficient room for individual manoeuvre and on the other, to use Michael Jackson's words, *'to have a nasty little pin pricking away'*.

The need to win should not be underestimated as a driving force. Unsurprisingly, a number of comparisons were made which take us back to individual achievements. Ruth McCall and Daniel Libeskind spoke of Michelangelo, Michael Jackson described the tactics of top seeded tennis players and Brian Pitman used both golfing and sailing analogies.

Competition is a constant spur. Having an enemy on your heels can build solidarity and sharpen the mind. It also generates a sense of difference and can encourage an organisation to do the unexpected. A creative organisation is likely to wrong foot a less flexible and nimble competitor by its ability to duck and dive when everything is fluid and fast changing.

Creativity American style

Any broad-ranging discussion on creativity, bravery and risk-taking will feed off comparisons with America. American culture and business are thought to be mutually supportive. Americans readily acknowledge that capitalism is fuelled by wanting to be the winner in the marketplace. They are quite unembarrassed by being openly good at managing, selling and marketing; in fact, they positively relish the hard end of business. And, most importantly, they accept that having a go will result in mistakes. Less fear of failure makes them more likely to take a chance and back an idea. Americans are more likely to look at a business idea in terms of what they might gain, not what they might lose.

There was broad agreement that Americans have a more intuitive understanding of the process of wealth creation and in general have established a business culture and environment that is more conducive to, and supportive of, creativity. The Americans recognise it earlier and know how to make it deliver commercially. This doesn't mean, however, that they are intrinsically more creative; if anything, adverse circumstances and obstacles can result in more inventive problem solving because it requires digging deeper for creative solutions.

Creativity the British way

The social environment that surrounds acts of creativity is crucial. In Britain you rarely get more than one chance to succeed, and whilst we can be intolerant of failure, we also seem to have a problem with people who do too well. The British can be both envious and find wealth distasteful in equal measure. Yet the entrepreneurs interviewed in this book were unashamedly interested in money and in the financial value of the businesses that they had founded. For them it created a virtuous circle: making money allowed them to do interesting things with that money. They saw wealth creation benefiting society and were keen to engage in it as often as opportunity allowed. They believed that the more traditional British new business model was less ambitious: the founders would sell out earlier in the cycle and use the money to fund less commercial activities that would be considered socially, and therefore intrinsically, more worthwhile.

That business is not a good use of time remains a persistent social prejudice. The tendency has been for the ablest graduates either to remain in academia or to move into the professions or civil service. And the latter work environments are not, on the whole, famous for encouraging creativity, innovation or risk taking. Yet the characteristics which are still valued among the educated in Britain, such as tolerance, lack of prejudice and cultural openness, combined with the communication advantages bestowed by the English language when it comes to expressing ideas, provide a good starting point for commercial creativity.

Signs of change

There was a shared belief amongst several of the contributors that an entrepreneurial culture could be instilled if you started young enough and educated for it. They believed that young children could be excited and inspired by the creative possibilities of business. Whilst some felt that this should start at primary school, Hermann Hauser's example of how enthusiastically the Business Plan run by Cambridge University's Entrepreneurial Society was received demonstrates the benefits to be had later, as a part of tertiary education. Overall, contributors want business to become aspirational once more.

This may be happening, however, at an informal rather than institutional level. In the 1980s there was lavish behaviour in the City and in industries such as advertising. Strong personalities and tales of barrow boys made good were legion. And for each new Porsche out on the streets there were a thousand more bright students clamouring to join these sectors.

These days the headlines are full of technology and dot.com millionaire profiles. Students can see the possibilities for making money and the attraction of creating their own business. It is part of the culture that surrounds them. As a result, recent graduates are becoming much more interested in getting involved in business start-ups. Even if it is not the first thing you do, it may well be the second, causing more established companies to think harder about creating the conditions that will retain their brightest, most radical employees. A number of contributors, several of them from large organisations, acknowledged that they hoped their children might experience the excitement of a start-up or an early stage company. And a start-up is, after all, an act of creativity in itself.

So, times are changing and creativity is alive and well within Britain, on an individual and collective level. Traditionally Britain has been good at entrepreneurship and professional creativity; it has been less good at organising for it. Rob Goffee remarked that as a nation, Britain is temperamentally happier with less structured, more flexible organisations which have suited professional and creative forms of work. This foundation, coupled with some of the developments discussed in these pages – larger businesses interfacing more with small ones; management empowering greater flexibility and creativity within their organisations; and technology driving new, more creative ways of working together – would all suggest that our time may have come. But, to use the words of Chairman Mao when he was asked to comment on the French Revolution as re-counted by Christopher Frayling, 'it's a little too early to tell'.

What follows are twenty edited transcripts from conversations which took place with the contributors over April and May 2000. I am enormously grateful to all of them for the willingness with which they gave their time and for the eloquence with which they warmed to the theme. I am particularly grateful for the way in which they all took such a broad perspective on the subject allowing for deeper insights which are applicable across business and thereby making my job as editor so much easier. I hope you enjoy reading the contributions as much as I enjoyed my conversations with the contributors. These are their words and this is their book.

Acknowledgements

I must thank four people without whom there would be no book. Firstly, Chris Powell, Chairman of BMP DDB, who seeded the idea and commissioned the book. In the enlightened tradition of his agency, Chris felt a compelling urge to broaden the debate on commercial creativity. Secondly, Julia Hobsbawm, founding partner of Hobsbawm Macaulay Communications, who believed in the project from the start and catapulted it from concept to execution. Thirdly, Ella Bennathan from Hobsbawm Macaulay Communications, who organised all the interviews and photographs with tireless energy. She was attentive to the smallest detail and a constant support. Finally, I must thank Sarah Jane Costello from BMP DDB, who had the thankless but crucial task of transcribing the tapes. Her sharp ear and quick fingerwork provided the foundations on which this book was built.

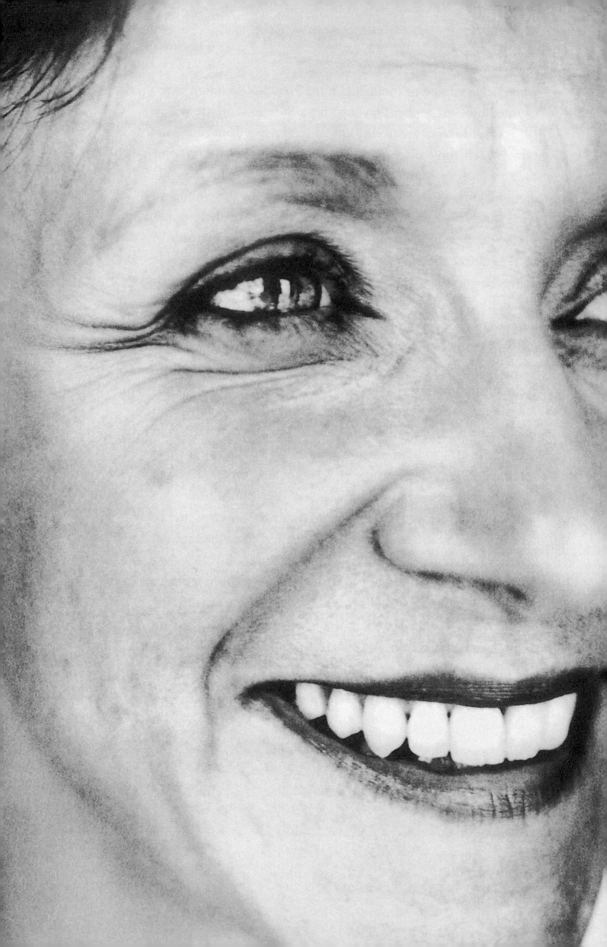

Helen Alexander was appointed Chief Executive of The Economist Group in January 1997. She joined the Group in 1985 as marketing manager for The Economist. In 1993 she became Managing Director of the Economist Intelligence Unit. The profits of this wholly owned subsidiary increased sevenfold by the end of 1996 when she left to succeed Marjorie Scardino in her current post. She is also a non-executive director of BT plc and of Northern Foods plc. She is married with three children under the age of 10.

Helen Alexander

Almost every business has creative people within it, and is therefore to some extent a creative business. The term 'creative industries' is wrong because it fails to cover all the creativity that goes on in other industries. What matters is people and their ability to think creatively. I believe it's possible to have lateral thinkers in all areas of an organisation – in accounts, in personnel, in management.

The more creative the person, the more opinionated they will be, and the more capable of taking data and turning it into an idea. These are people who need the opportunity to express their ideas. They need to feel that their voice can be heard and that they can make an impact. It's crucial for managers to listen to these people and to allow their ideas to be shaped by others.

However, this is anathema in a command-and-control environment where 'what we are going to do' doesn't warrant any discussion. The characteristics of the leader matter too; if he or she is too certain, or the kind of person that works everything out in their head before saying anything, then the opportunity people perceive for changing that idea is very limited. Having an immediate superior who is not able to listen or take things on board is a real barrier to innovation and creativity. If you are in a position of responsibility then being open to ideas is critical for the creativity of the people within the organisation.

Collaboration is part of this, because the best ideas are usually formed from bits of other people's good ideas. It seems perfectly natural to me that people should be able to work in partnership much more easily than in the past. There's a major and highly significant mind-shift going on from 'that's a competitor' to 'no, that's a potential partner'. We have a recent example of that with someone who was about to leave us to work for another organisation, but for him the more creative and motivating idea was to work across the two organisations while remaining employed by us. Now we're collaborating and all benefiting from each other's input. No one's the loser.

These creative partnerships have more potential in some industries than others. For instance, in technology and in the communication industries, where customers care about what they are getting but are not so worried about how it has arrived. If they are not able to distinguish between sources of supply, and those suppliers are in some way working together, then the customer can benefit. It's exciting as new models challenge the status quo.

Within all industries, however, there are companies for whom challenging the status quo has always been part of their corporate culture. It's less to do with what they produce, or the nature of their customers, and more to do with being a function of the way things are done.

In our own business, we have tried to encapsulate in words the kind of environment that we want and we came up with *a network of world class media professionals.* The word network is important. It isn't the same as a team because it isn't about roles acting together. It's more fluid and has more flexibility than that. It allows for movement from one assignment or one job to another. But it needs to rest upon a bedrock of something that really works. Part of managing people who have good ideas and can have big ideas, is understanding the frustration – which I suspect is more acute amongst those people – when things don't work properly. What is essential is respect for those professionals in other fields who get on with doing the basics well. That provides the springboard that allows others to function creatively. So in our industry it is important that all the basic things are done brilliantly. We want the best people who are skilled in those functions so that others can go off and do what they are good at.

I also think size matters. Even within big organisations it is easier to manage creativity in smaller units. What matters is that people feel that they are part of a community where they can be heard. I know someone who owns a business where every time he adds 40 more people he spins them off into another business unit. He works to a very clear mechanism. But it would be crass to take a number and apply it across all industries. It's to do with the group you can identify with.

Geography also plays a part, in the sense that you need to create space to have some perspective. And it helps if you are further away from the centre. That's one of the privileges of being Chief Executive, you can go outside the organisation and look in, helicopter-like.

Because there was a concern that we were losing ideas within the company, we did some quite formal work to try and track the life of an idea. We looked at how many ideas we had, not just tiny ideas but quite big ideas – and whether they got to the next stage, i.e. somebody's immediate boss, or whether they got serious discussion at company level. Also whether they got the resources to do research or business planning and whether they got to market or not. Of course the number that you start with is many times greater than the number that you end up with. But it is very important to understand that process in order to be sure that you are capturing what you can from within the organisation. Having the resource to examine the implementation of ideas is very important. Proper implementation may be the less fashionable end of business activity, but ideas are nothing without it.

It's very fashionable to talk about learning from mistakes, especially with the benefit of hindsight. It also depends on the degree of the mistake. It's hard for companies to make big mistakes and applaud them. When the scale is relatively small, then it is possible, but still difficult to recognise and put down to individual and corporate experience. However, as people look at their careers in terms of what they have learnt, taking responsibility for mistakes has the potential to be very positive.

I also believe that praise and recognition is extremely important. It may sound a bit of a cliché but it's something we need to remember in this country and I think all too often it goes out of the life of a company. I don't think that's the case in America. In America it's 'congratulations' for getting up in the morning.

Creativity is driven by direct and intense competition. Markets impose a clear short-term focus for companies and I think creativity has to work alongside that. The relationship between creativity and making money is intricate and complex but I do think that the two are inextricably linked. If a competitor is doing something you have to respond – even if you choose to do nothing it is still a sharpening of the mind. It's a constant challenge having somebody at your heels. We try to think what we would do, if we were starting something, to compete against ourselves.

Having something to push against is an important characteristic of a creative organisation. It is full of people with opinions challenging the prevailing thinking. What appears aggressive to an outsider is merely an idea being tested – not everyone likes that kind of environment.

I don't like new words such as 'co-opetition', but to have people who are your customers, your suppliers, your partners and your competitors is perfectly possible. Everybody knows which hat is being worn at the time, but it makes it a more sophisticated game if everybody is aware of all the elements rather than somebody playing one tune. I think you get a better result if there is a broad picture, which is definitely the case in the convergence industries.

If someone wanted to work in a business environment which they felt had a real creative buzz about it, I think you would point them to a highly competitive, relatively young and informal environment. And on the basis of those generalisations that would probably lead me to one of today's internet companies. This may not be the case longer-term, but I think there is so much change in that area that if somebody was bored with their job, they could get a shot in the arm doing that. And then if you want to go one stage further I'd suggest doing it outside your own originating culture, say in California or Italy or Asia.

Regulation makes a difference and when seeking commercial creativity the conventional view is to look to deregulated countries like the US or Hong Kong. But even in environments like Europe, where there is a very intricate form of social and financial regulation, getting under the net or around the framework is producing its own creative solutions. I think the European picture is promising in the sense that there are the people here who not only have the idea but also have the creativity to make it happen in quite a difficult environment. It makes for some very subtle innovations that are at least as interesting as those in the US overall. An example here would be retail property development where the creative approaches being adopted are partly in response to the regulatory framework and are more interesting on the whole than what is happening on the continent.

I think that there are positive changes afoot in Britain. In the regulatory environment of both tax and law we are starting to take some of the best aspects from America. Nor is business education seen as a second rate set of studies these days. A lot of secondary schools now run a scheme called Young Enterprise where teams set up a business with a company secretary, a chief executive and so on, and they take money for the products they make. It gives even those people who will never be anywhere near business some knowledge and, I hope, some respect for it.

However, tertiary business education (the MBA), is still an uneasy thing in British culture. I think it is still seen as smart-Alec, know-it-all, and that will only be changed by the number of people who have MBAs and who are good at what they do.

As we move away from a 2–3 subject A-level system, the breadth of people who stay at school until they are 18 will definitely improve. There is also a small increase in the number of people who are doing an international baccalaureate rather than going through the English system. It's a sign that people recognise that breadth is really important. Scientific education is hugely important as well. There are too many people, myself included, who have too little scientific preparation for the way in which we think.

Diversity and breadth both need to be reflected in the workforce and that needs constant vigilance. It's everybody's responsibility, and particularly the chief executive's responsibility, to ensure a creative range of people. Just because you don't like what someone says doesn't mean they shouldn't work for you. It's important that people and the organisation are constantly challenged and tested. If you are not tested inside, then you are not going to be as sharp (or as commercially successful) as you might be outside.

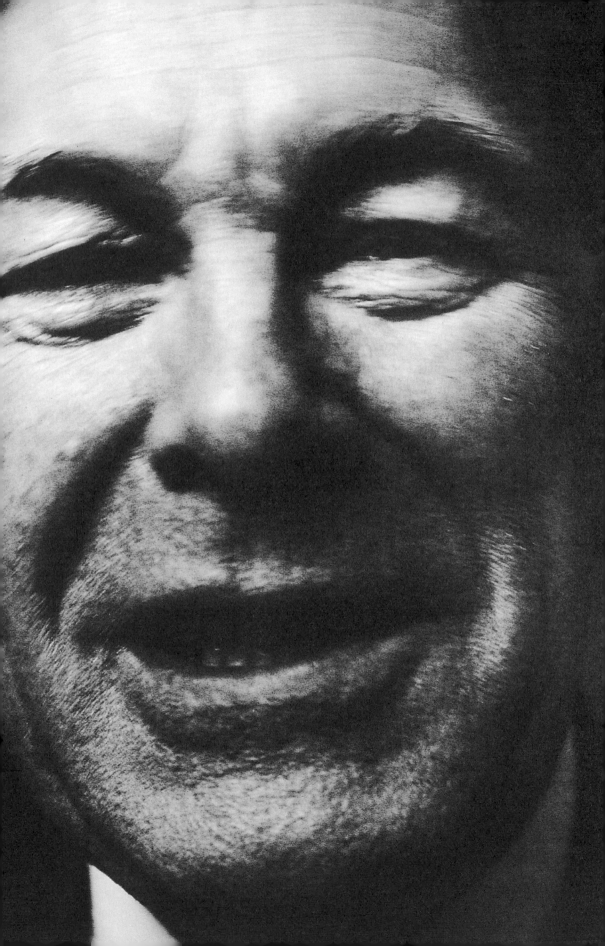

R oger Cairns is a scientist and works as a petroleum engineer.
He obtained six patents as a research chemist with BP where
he led numerous innovation projects both in Research and
Exploration & Production. He was then a founder member of
Trafalgar House Oil and Gas before becoming Managing Director
of Hardy Oil & Gas in 1989 which, during his time as MD, increased its market capitalisation sixfold from £60 million to £365
million. Since 1997 he has acted as a consultant to the petroleum industry and is currently Chairman and CEO of CEDAR International plc, a new concept oil company with the objective of
co-operatively developing oil and gas assets owned and operated by
national oil companies.

**Roger
Cairns**

think there are two sorts of creativity. One sort is when people are looking for something entirely new or for a totally new way of doing something. And I think that's generally regarded as the creative bit – if you end up patenting something. The other sort of creativity, which is generally much more prevalent and not so recognised, is when people think outside the box and take existing knowledge and things but put them together in a way that's not been done before or not been applied in that particular industry.

Here's an example: I was talking to someone about a water injection system that you can put on the seabed. He believed that it was all existing technology, but I pointed out that in essence it was existing know-how; the technology was new because what had happened was that three things had been put together in a way that no one had thought of before. It's a bit like a radio set. The difference between a radio set and the bits of kit that make it up, is that a radio set actually does something. You make those connections that create something new but it's not new from a fundamental point of view. The creative step is often not the science. The creative step is applying the science. There's an awful lot of science that never sees the light of day until somebody actually says *'Ah, but if we put that with that with that, we'd have a steam engine'*.

There is a clear distinction between innovation and creative thinking. Innovation would be where you come up with something entirely new. Like a rotary drill bit instead of the percussion drill. The traditional view is that in oil and gas production it is more about innovation than creative thinking. But in fact it's absolutely the reverse.

Let me give you another example. In Alaska we were drilling through permafrost. One of the fundamental problems we had was how to make sure the well didn't just sink into the ground. You drill down, you put the casing in, but it's just metal pipe and as soon as the hot oil starts coming up the pipe it melts the permafrost and everything just sinks. We realised what we needed was low conductivity cement. Then I thought why not put foaming agent in the cement so it foams and forms a honeycomb and because it's low conductivity the heat won't get through permanently? That's not actually innovative in the sense that its brand new; foaming agents are well known, cement is well known. But the creative bit is applying it in a real life situation and actually making a difference. Without that we would never have had any producing wells in Alaska.

There is an area of industrial research which can be driven by changes in legislation; for example low sulphur diesel or unleaded fuel driven by emissions standards. The research is on the product, but how do we continue to make this product while still managing to meet whatever the criteria happen to be? And I would argue that in most industries, certainly in our industry, Oil and Gas, 90% of the research is like that. It's trying to make the processes more efficient or the product a little better. It's incremental change, not step change.

And then about 10% is on what you might call fundamental research. British industry has, in my experience, been uneasy with this. Management sees fundamental research as swallowing up vast amounts of money and it's difficult to judge whether this is wisely spent year on year.

Bell Telephones is a very good example of how fundamental research ought to be done. Back in the early 50s they had a whole group looking at how materials conduct electricity on the basis that their main business was sending electrons down wires. You might think it's a telephone, but they saw it as these copper wires that were carrying signals that they could improve on. So they had this whole group looking at how materials conduct electricity, just as a fundamental project. What came out of that wasn't a better way of doing it, because that was fibre optics eventually and invented elsewhere, but the transistor. They had hit upon the fact that some materials are actually semi-conductive. Look at what it led to – everything!

The fundamental research was done in an area that was important for the company, but without prejudice to what the outcome might be. I feel that one of the problems in British industry is that we try to prescribe our research. We tell them to research what we think we really want to know. Instead of saying for example, *'what we'd like to do is make long chain molecules and find a better way of hooking them together'*, we could say, *'could you look into the whole business of how molecules actually join up and what is it that drives them to be in this shape, or that shape, as a fundamental project'*. We need to have more faith. By and large things that don't do the right thing are just not taken any further.

We all know the saying that 'necessity is the mother of invention'. I just don't think that's right. Take radar as an example. The theory of radar was done in the 1920s – that if you were to send out two radio waves and then let the reflections interact, you could actually locate where an object was. That had been done but everybody said *'so what?'*. And then the war comes along and people say we would like some way of knowing where the enemy aircraft are. They didn't suddenly invent radar, they applied the existing science. Same with the jet engine in 1932 – people had no need for faster planes at first. I think what they do is they open a bottom drawer and pull out something that they've been looking for a way of applying for the last 20 years. If they'd gone looking for new scientific principles they would have found the war was over before they'd invented anything.

In peacetime, the equivalent is to know there's a market. A guaranteed market or a big prize spurs creativity and innovation. What you can do is to incentivise the market. You can say, if you can get that right, you can have 10 years of a very useful patent on it or 10 years of income and you can make yourself a ton of money. Then I think people are prepared to put the time, money and effort in.

You also need people who can see things with a completely different eye – people who will look at a cube and describe it from the corner, where it looks quite different from the usual face-on view. They are often the people who are just new in, because everything looks different to them – *'why do you do it that way? why don't you do it this way?'* Yet if you're in a hierarchical system, it's the newest or most junior person who gets squashed – *'listen lad, we don't need your ideas – I've been around the patch for 20 years and managed just fine'*. You need an environment that encourages people to voice their opinions without fear and where you're encouraged to share your ideas. Where people are judged on the quality of what they do and not on their output. Everybody wants to feel that they've somehow been part and parcel of the discovery of a new idea, so if you're only going to judge by the end point, not by the quality of what's been done in the research, that makes for a lot of backbiting and politics.

If you have the germ of an idea and you build it as a team, nobody claims to have had the idea because all of you have somehow constructed it. You interacted in the right way, you acted as team players pulling for the company and not for yourselves. You need smaller units, a flat structure, access to the senior level, and genuine delegation. Otherwise it can be like treading through treacle to try and get anywhere. You're no longer playing a creative game but a political game.

To collaborate well you need a shared goal. If you don't have that then however good the collaboration looks on paper, it just won't work. And you need to make sure you share the profit – that's the hard bit – sharing the prize. You don't always need mergers, just the collaboration where it matters. Industry is too territorial so it happens far less than it should.

One of the core areas where British industry does incredibly badly is in collaboration with universities; because the universities don't share the prize in general. If there's a university/industry collaboration it's always industry that says it should have the patent. If the university shared in those royalties it would not be so beholden to company interests. In America the universities insist on it. If they're collaborating and sharing the prize then the goals become aligned and everyone wants something that works, that actually does something real.

We're a nation that is terribly scathing about business – it's considered much better to be an FRS than a commercially successful scientist. The problem with things that work is that they all seem to be so obvious. There is a sense in which technology is taken for granted and no longer seems creative. I think we have a culture in which we reward people for being worthy rather than useful.

*P*hilip Dowson was the founding architectural partner of Arup Associates. When it began in 1963 it represented a radical move towards a multi-disciplinary practice of architecture and engineering. He remained a senior partner of the Ove Arup Partnership until his retirement in 1990 and is still a consultant to the firm.

He was made a CBE in 1969 and in 1980 was knighted for services to architecture. In 1981 he received the Royal Gold Medal for Architecture. In 1993 he was elected President of the Royal Academy of Arts and remained in this position until the end of 1999. At present he is engaged as Director of Design for Battersea Power Station and Site Development.

Philip Dowson

I have spent my life trying to knock down organisational pyramids. Pyramids are impenetrable. To penetrate a pyramid you need to devise a complicated route called bureaucracy. The point of the horizontal structure at Arup was that one person, with a brilliant idea, could penetrate the sky immediately. There was nothing to block them.

The whole notion of Arup was the creation of a 'Trust'. No one therefore owned anything, no one could get rich at the expense of others and profits were all ploughed back for research and development. It was also totally multi-disciplinary. You avoid systematisation, because so much progress, especially scientific, is the result of different disciplines working together and accidental things being allowed to happen. It is where disciplines overlap that interesting things so often occur. Controlling things is about removing the accidental and that's the one thing you don't want within observant creativity. It needs to remain alive to surprise.

You shouldn't have too much order. Look at Picasso who refused to live in a modern, clean house because as an artist he wanted to be surrounded by the maximum diversity for cross fertilisation and accidental relationships.

Managing this culture is the most difficult thing of all because democracy is cruel – if someone is no good he is judged by his peers, and if you have an open society you get a very competitive environment. You therefore need smaller units – little villages. We worked in project groups of about 20 people with six professional disciplines in each group and an administrator who would oil the wheels and deal with the finances. We had about five of these groups in Arup Associates and that worked well.

The danger is that you can still end up with a number of baronies, and corporate line management emerges with corporate structures. Security and complacency then set in and you find people sitting back and growing weight around their waists. You need to be vigilant. Corporate structure is ultimately about creating security, yet creativity has got nothing to do with security. In fact security often inhibits creativity. You get much more creativity when you're hungry and you need to survive.

There's an extraordinary notion around at present which suggests that human judgement can be replaced by some mythical idea of administrative infallibility. Administration layered upon administration prevents originality. We see the grey results all around us.

I think a good organisation eliminates alibis. When you have a situation where people do not feel that they are personally responsible for what they do it snuffs out creativity. Creativity, imagination and invention can be a real threat to your superior in a corporate structure. If you're right you might get ahead. I hate corporate structures, they creep in like cancers.

You need the mavericks to break the shackles and challenge the obvious. In medieval courts you had the jester – someone to challenge the King. But where there aren't Kings and there aren't pyramids, you don't have the same problem.

The most important thing is to recognise creativity and, when it is recognised, to back it. For this to happen it is essential to keep the melting pot of ideas bubbling over. It can be very insecure but it allows you to catch ideas on the wing. And there has to be an element of vision for creativity to take flight.

Pyramids are death to creativity.

Charles Dunstone

I n 1989, at the age of 25, Charles Dunstone set up The Carphone Warehouse with £6,000 in the bank. He recognised that the mobile phone market was geared to corporate buyers and energetically addressed the needs of small business, the self-employed and the public.

Today Carphone Warehouse is Europe's largest independent retailer of mobile communications with over 300 stores in the UK, 800 outlets across Europe and over 4,500 employees. In 1999 group sales were £697 million with operating profits of £30.4 million.

The company is a heavy investor in new wireless technology and internet opportunities. It has its own e-retail centre, it has launched a free ISP service in partnership with BT and it was one of the first retailers to launch with Open, the interactive shopping channel.

I hate the idea of having to 'sell' or having to convince someone that they ought to buy something. As a result we have two rules when we hire people at Carphone Warehouse. One is you can't work for us if you've ever worked for a mobile phone company. The other is that you can't work for us if you've worked in direct sales before. We avoid people who've perfected their closing techniques.

The core idea behind Carphone Warehouse is to attract people and to make sure there is no reason why they shouldn't buy from us. We win a lot of business because we disarm people by saying, *'Look if you're not sure, have a think about it, you don't have to buy it today'*. My impression of salesmanship is urging people to buy something ahead of them making the decision themselves. Our aim is to make it as easy as possible for you to make the choice. It is essential that every single person who leaves Carphone Warehouse having bought something feels that they made the decision.

I think the skill we have developed is one of sensitivity towards how people like things presented to them and how they like to buy things. That's what we're good at, and what a lot of retailers are bad at. Many are strangely disconnected from the act of shopping. I don't think the people who run Boots, for example, know what it's like to go and shop in Boots. They have a perception that is not that close to the reality. Too much of what happens in Boots is about making things work the best way for Boots, not the best way for their customers. We're by no means perfect at it, but I think we're better than most.

I believe some of the big business success stories of the last 10–15 years, Virgin Atlantic, Pret à Manger, Dyson, are due to people who have shown a much greater sensitivity to what it's like to buy, or use, their product or service.

The impression I have is that James Dyson went into a very established marketplace, that hadn't changed for years, and actually figured out what it was people hated about the product and really thought about the things that would make the product more functional and easier to use. His perspective is very customer driven. Apparently if you break a bit on your Dyson, they won't charge you. You don't have to mess around and find a parts centre. His approach is, *'here's my product, we think it's great but if you've got a problem with it please call us. If you've broken the little bit that connects the so and so to the so and so, don't worry we'll pop one in the post to you'*.

Meanwhile Julian Metcalfe at Pret à Manger completely understood that people wanted interesting, varied, nicely presented things to eat at lunchtime that were still quick and easy to buy. A Marks & Spencer sandwich and a Pret à Manger sandwich are leagues apart. Julian Metcalfe worked out that putting lots of filling in and making sure it goes right to the edge of the bread so it looks as if it's bursting is very appealing, but not very expensive. I suspect that the people at Marks & Spencer worry more about the logistics – the refrigerated lorries that are delivering the sandwiches and the forecasting system that works out how many prawns to buy. And what Pret à Manager has done to M&S by focussing on the front customer end with sandwiches, The Gap has done with clothes.

There's too much focus in a lot of businesses on the logistics in the back office which drives a *'can't do'* attitude rather than an attitude of, *'we have to do it, it's what the customer wants, so how are we going to make it happen?'*. All too often the business is being determined by the back-end process and no one has the energy or the will to step outside, turn around and look at themselves from the outside.

Central to our business is the belief that you have to satisfy customers' needs and then you have to *delight* them. A good example would be that if you buy a mobile phone from us, you would expect it to be priced competitively. So we have to go and study what everyone else is charging first, and make sure our prices are competitive. Then we say to you, *'if you can find it cheaper, don't worry, we'll beat that price'*. And if, seven days after you bought it, you find it cheaper elsewhere, then we'll give you 110% of the difference. We regard that as satisfying your need to buy a product and not be ripped off or have to pay a premium for it. So at that level, we're sorting out customer satisfaction.

Then we go one stage further, which we class as customer delight. If you find that what you bought for £100, is now only worth £60 after two months, you'd still feel a bit cheated. So, three and a half months after each phone purchase, we write to every customer comparing the price they paid for it to the price we're now selling it at, and if it's fallen in price then we send them a voucher for the difference. People are just blown away by that. It may seem unnecessary, but the imagination and courage it takes drives our business. We get huge pleasure out of the thought of our customers opening their post and spitting their cornflakes over the breakfast table in astonishment.

For Dixons or Boots it is totally beyond reason that, having made our margin, we should then give it back to the customer later. But actually, when we do the sums on how people redeem it and what they spend it on, we find it works to our advantage. There is an argument for direct mailing our customers at that stage anyway but it's a massively customer-centric piece of communication because it acknowledges how people feel when they've just bought a phone, a camera, a TV or a PC and they open the paper, and see it cheaper.

Ideas are the lifeblood of the organisation, so we pay everyone who works here for their suggestions on how we can improve the business regardless of whether or not they are implemented and even if they are completely barking. We want a culture where ideas can flood in so the only rule is that we don't pay for it if the suggestion has already been made.

I was looking at two suggestions this morning. We've always had difficulty cleaning the screens of our tills and one person found a camera cloth that works. It's pretty mundane at one level but it is a problem that needed solving, so now we can all go out and buy these cloths. Then at another level, someone is suggesting that we allow people to suspend their phone service for a sabbatical period and then come back and resume it. That is potentially possible, but it requires an enormous amount of negotiation with our suppliers because it's their airtime. So that idea will need to be pursued in partnership.

Other ideas come from observing what others do. Some of us were in a restaurant in America a little while ago where they give you a pager so you can have a drink in the bar and then they page you when your table is ready. We have places in shopping centres where you can take your phone to have it fixed while you wait. The restaurant experience made us think we should give people pagers so they can carry on shopping in Blue Water or wherever, and when the phone's fixed, we can page them to come back and pick it up. It's really a case of translating smart things that other people have worked out and applying them to different situations.

As a culture, we like doing unconventional things. It helps that our main competitor is Dixons, which is very traditional. They are incredibly efficient both logistically and operationally but they don't believe in giving the customer anything more than they need to. It's all sell, sell, sell – never genuinely cheaper, just lots of crass retail promotions. It makes us revel in being completely different.

We are the only people in the marketplace who sell all the networks and our staff are genuinely free to recommend what they want – they earn exactly the same amount of money regardless. There's no prescription, we don't say that if someone comes in and their circumstances are this, then you should sell them that. It's completely up to the individual in the store to advise and that gives them self-respect and pride. They're consultants not sales machines, and people pay them for their consultancy by buying phones from them. They take pride in their impartiality. If they go and work anywhere else, they'll get a fax on a Friday saying there's double money if you sell Cellnet this weekend.

I think the Dixons way is still the retailing norm. Asda is unusual in having a more entrepreneurial culture. They've empowered the people that work in the business a great deal more than is usual and they've made it fun to work there. They've also tried to embrace customers with a number of new ideas, like having drive-in cinemas in their car parks, having meeters and greeters and singles nights. Some of them may be gimmicks but that doesn't really matter because it all makes Asda a more interesting and fun place and builds a positive feeling. It gives me a more positive feeling about them as a supermarket because if they're being creative and having all these ideas in areas that don't relate directly to their core business then my assumption is that they're being at least as creative in the rest of their business. It's about the way you approach things; it would be easier for them just to say it's always cheaper at Asda but they want to go further and make me feel they really want my custom. I think it's a good fit with Wal Mart who have always been pro-active in the community.

Tesco have done it too but perhaps less overtly. Whenever Tesco said they were going to do something, it was always really well implemented. Sainsbury's, on the other hand would make similar claims but you'd go in-store and it wouldn't happen. They simply couldn't get their organisation to deliver. That's when you end up with a Boots or WH Smith situation where you don't offer things because they are too difficult to implement. You get into this terrible spiral of never having any new initiatives.

In America there is this home improvement store called Home Depot. They've just taken the home improvement market by storm with simple customer focussed ideas. For example, they have expert helpers in all the sections. If you're planning to fit a shower and you go to B&Q or Homebase, you look at bits of pipes and shower trays and you've got to work out how to connect it all together when you get home. At Home Depot there's someone there to help you work it all through. You buy all the same stuff, but when you get home it all works, because someone helped you buy it and explained what to do with it. As a result you have a much better home improvement experience which means you're more confident about going back next time. It seems so obvious.

Maybe there is more of a sense now that the person at the top of the business has to be accountable to their customers in a way that they weren't traditionally. I give customers my personal e-mail and direct line so they can speak to me because I think that's really important. Not just important for our customers but as a signal to everyone in the organisation that we're in this together. We're all accountable when something goes wrong, whether or not it's our fault, and we've got to resolve it together.

It makes the organisation more integrated, more meritocratic and less hierarchical. We don't think in terms of the shop floor and the managers, we're all in it together to sell phones and to keep our customers happy and that's what makes us all tick. The scale that we've achieved has given us a better team spirit and focus than we've ever had because size gives people confidence. The people here really believe what we're about because we've done well and delivered it.

We measure our employee turnover, which is about 18%. I'm quite relaxed about that because we have lots of people who leave university and use us as a stepping stone to building a career and that's fine. What I really focus on is how many leave us to go and work for one of our direct competitors and in the last 18 months only three people have left Carphone Warehouse to do that. That is the acid test because if you go and work for one of our competitors, then we've failed because you've decided there's someone else out there doing something better than us. It is the same with our customers – if we are getting it right, then there should never be any reason for them to go anywhere else.

Having said all that, we're still young and we still get lots of things wrong. I get nervous that because we're seen as a successful retail case history that we're in danger of being put on a pedestal. People seem to study us more than I feel comfortable with. No one who founded this company had ever run a business or worked in retail before. So everything we've done has been instinctive. We figured things out for ourselves and we were lucky, it worked well. The danger is that if you get made into a role model, people just try to mimic you, they don't necessarily go through the thought process for themselves. What we did was appropriate for us, at the time, in our market. If people embrace the idea of putting the customer first then there are lots of ways to execute it.

There's no mystique. It's about observation and pragmatism. It all comes down to common sense at the end of the day – a great British quality.

Chris Evans

*C*hris Evans is one of Europe's leading biotechnology entrepreneurs. He was the founder of Merlin Ventures and now
leads Merlin Biosciences. He has successfully created and
commercialised a number of technology start-ups, three of which
– Chiroscience Group, Celsis International and Toad – are now
publicly listed. In 1995 he was awarded the OBE for services to
biotechnology and in 1999 he was placed 4th in the Enterprise Top
100. He holds Professorships at Imperial College, Liverpool,
Exeter and Manchester Universities where he lectures regularly. He
is an advisor on biotechnology and start-up companies to the government and travels the country to promote enterprise and awareness of science and high technology business for the future of the
UK.

I am a scientist who became an entrepreneur. Over the last 10 years, I've built around 17 companies: most are in biomedicine and biotechnology. They were all my babies at some stage, and so I know each one of them from the roots all the way up. I've floated four of them and the rest are still private. It's a case of pathological, serial enterprise. I won't stop now, I like what I do.

Merlin, which I recently formed, is a specialist venture capital company run by a team of entrepreneurs. I think it's the new breed of venture capitalism, based more on the American model, where real input comes from people who have made their own money and built their own businesses, rather than simply having MBA graduates manage other people's money.

In my area it is fundamental that the science is brilliant. You need to be very creative about using science to discover and invent but you need to be just as creative to know how to exploit it. The latter needs a different kind of creativity – bringing it to maturity, financing and building the company. And it is the management team and vision that makes the real difference. You need to see about 7 to 10 years ahead in order to develop something from scratch through to completion in this area.

Creative and smart are the same word for me. You've got to be very smart about following your nose when you discover and invent in the first place. But for me, now, the creativity really counts when you've got all that discovery going on and you're building a pipeline of new projects. When I created Chiroscience we had a large number of projects in asthma, arthritis, cancer, inflammation and anaesthesia. These were all different research and clinical projects running in parallel. All the clinical trials were in completely different hospitals with completely different patients. And simultaneously you're trying to finance the company, talk to the City, float at £100 million plus and convince the big drug companies to take on your discoveries. Managing a project needs real creativity: how you motivate the scientists and clinicians, how you set up the trials, how you sell it to the drug company, how you sell it to the City to raise money, and how you convince the doctors. It requires creative deals on many levels.

The whole process is oozing with opportunities to be creative and imaginative in my opinion. But so few companies take advantage of it. You get managers who've come out of the big drug companies and who are all trained in the same way and, all do the same thing. It's not so much that what they are doing is wrong, it's just that it isn't necessarily always smart or innovative enough.

Management teams can lose sight of what they're trying to achieve and can fail to look ahead. One of my young, private companies may think they'll just raise money from the City. But what happens if they don't give you any? You need to think ahead. The company could merge with another one in a similar position with a view to floating. It could merge with an existing public company to access new money. The company could be sold and the profits returned to the shareholders, with the new buyer taking the drugs into the marketplace. Or the company could raise money itself through private equity. Management should be thinking about all these options, not just one. In essence that's part of the role I perform – to help them be creative and lateral. I'm in there looking at the big picture. I can see my little company, which maybe didn't exist two years ago, worth £50 million today but I want it to be worth at least £500 million in ten years' time.

It is helpful to be at some distance so long as you're well briefed. Take one of the companies I helped to create, which has just made a very major breakthrough. I'm not the Chairman or a Director, but I have turned up at the odd meeting and suggested that they should go for a stock market listing now – not in two years' time – because they were no longer the company they thought they were. I told them that I felt they were extremely valuable, far more valuable than either they or anybody else had realised. From a distance I could see this little private company with an unknown value but with extraordinary science. Once you've made the breakthrough you need to throw money at it to develop it. I suggested to them to get into the public domain and raise £20 million to drive their science through into the clinic so patients could receive the drug as soon as possible. My job is sometimes providing that half an hour of confidence and inspiration, based on having done it over and over again. I am sure that some management teams turn around and say *'Phew, I'm glad Chris has left the room so we can get on with the work now'*. But some Chief Executives do react positively: *'You're absolutely right. Let's throw the windows open and go for it'*.

It's those small moments of inspiration that can change the direction. Sometimes it is strategic creativity, but with my scientific hat on I used to go into meetings and say, *'Why isn't this scientific project working?' 'Have we tried X or Y?'* or *'Why don't we put that molecule with that molecule?'* Other people can feed off a different way of looking at the problem and then take it forward in a new direction. It's about continuously throwing in as many ideas and scenarios as possible.

The solution is not always easy for me or for other people to see, so we must not belittle the issues. Life is complicated in these companies, but sometimes we overcomplicate it. I do get frustrated when people get bogged down in too much detail.

There are too many people in management who turn up at 9.00, sit behind a desk, and go through the motions of another good day in the office and maybe they did one or two good things. But they didn't do 12 good things and they didn't challenge themselves. Their ambition simply isn't there. It is a cultural issue. I could have remained in the US where the attitude is quite different but I chose not to.

For me it was reverse brain drain. I went over to the US in

the early 1980s for my research fellowship. I loved biotechnology and I knew what it was about as a science, but the commercial side hadn't occurred in Europe at all. I took some jobs over there and after two or three years I was offered a lot of money to invest in starting up my first company. But I said no, I'm going back to Britain. I missed the rugby, I missed the telly, I missed my pint of beer down at the pub on the corner and I missed my relatives and my mates from Port Talbot.

My British friends in the US said I was mad to be going back to dreary, grey, damp Britain, a crap salary and a City that would not tolerate me as a scientist and a maverick. But I saw that as the challenge for the rest of my life – I was going to *make* them respect me, I was going to set up my companies and ideas here, and *make* them work, drive them through, get to the top and not look back.

I sold my house and went up to Cambridge. We didn't know anyone there, but Cambridge was the mecca of science and I thought, if I'm going to build my first company successfully, it's going to be right there. Not in the Science Park – I couldn't afford that – I was just outside. I didn't think about what could go wrong, I just did it.

Two things motivated me. Firstly, I've always been interested in the creative side of science. So I wanted to create things, make them work my way and get them out into the market. It's not an ego thing because that quickly becomes self-fulfilling. It's because I like what I do and because I think it's a good thing to do.

Secondly, I know that to exploit what I create, I need money. Money makes it all go round. With money I can invest and I can make my own decisions and call the shots. I can invest my own money and other people will follow me. I have to have my own wealth at my disposal to do what I like.

I'm interested in wealth creation from science; I'm not interested in wealth creation from property, so I don't speculate in that area. I've invested well over £20 million of my own money to create things in medicine because that's what excites me. If I ever make a billion one day, I will re-invest at least £800 million in order to keep the whole cycle going. It's to keep the creativity and the challenge going. I love the excitement and the fun of creating new things from scratch. I take great joy in watching other people doing it as well, and saying *'I've got an idea, but you've got four ideas so let's put them together and I'll give you the money, you can kick it off and then it's your baby and by the way you could get very rich'*. It's great watching them develop. It's like helping them train your way and then not wanting them to stop.

Your upbringing does have a major bearing on whether or not you turn obstacles into opportunities. Too much comfort and security can work against enterprise. Entrepreneurs who come from working class backgrounds start with nothing. I never had enough money for the ice-cream van, I used to watch the other kids with ice creams. I had to figure out how to get one, so I used to go and pick berries and put them in a jar to sell them so I could buy an ice cream. If you are used to money, you don't have to work that out for yourself. If you speak to another 100 entrepreneurs from really poor backgrounds you'll find that they all did the same – they fought to find creative, imaginative ways around the obstacles. I now often joke that I've got more letters after my name than in it, not because I'm a scientific snob, but because I need these credentials and qualifications to do what I do.

If a bright kid here in the UK says he wants to start his own business his parents would say *'no don't do that – you could get a really good job in management at Marks & Spencer or in accountancy'*. Yet in America the parents are saying, *'George is going to set up his own company isn't that brilliant'*. Those years from 11–16 are crucial. That is when the confidence gets instilled and parents and teachers need to have a real dialogue about what their kids are good at and what needs to be encouraged, rather than just pushing them through the academic treadmill regardless. They should be going out into the world, bold and ambitious. Schools need to be more creative and challenging. They need to teach innovation and entrepreneurial skills so that students can go out into the world and do things differently. This hasn't been taught in schools or universities in my opinion. But in the last three years I've seen courses being set up. Some people say you can't teach people to be creative or entrepreneurial but I think you can. It's about giving young people confidence in themselves so that they can really go for it. They need to feel they can leave school or university and go in any number of directions rather than be predictable, because they know what they're doing.

Next week the National Enterprise campaign kicks off and I'm one of the ambassadors for it. There will be a string of events for children and students and I'll be doing a morning breakfast programme, a few interviews plus an event at No. 10.

The kids want to know about the money and the cars. We talk about my Ferrari Testarossa 512 TR and they want to know how fast it goes. But then you tell them that that's not what it's about. You tell them how it feels to invent medicines that save babies. You explain that that's what people like me do. That's how I make the money to buy a Ferrari and have fun. People like me have to invent these new medicines and that's what creates the value. One young student said to me *'Isn't that enough?'* which was a comment about my various achievements because it *is* enough for a lot of the people who work in my companies, but I need more, I need to be able to sell something else for another £100 million. I need the £10 million profit from one successful medicine to keep doing this because we've got a lot of diseases, such as cancer, arthritis, brain trauma and Parkinson's to deal with yet. It's good when you feel you can enthuse others and they can identify with who you are and what you're doing.

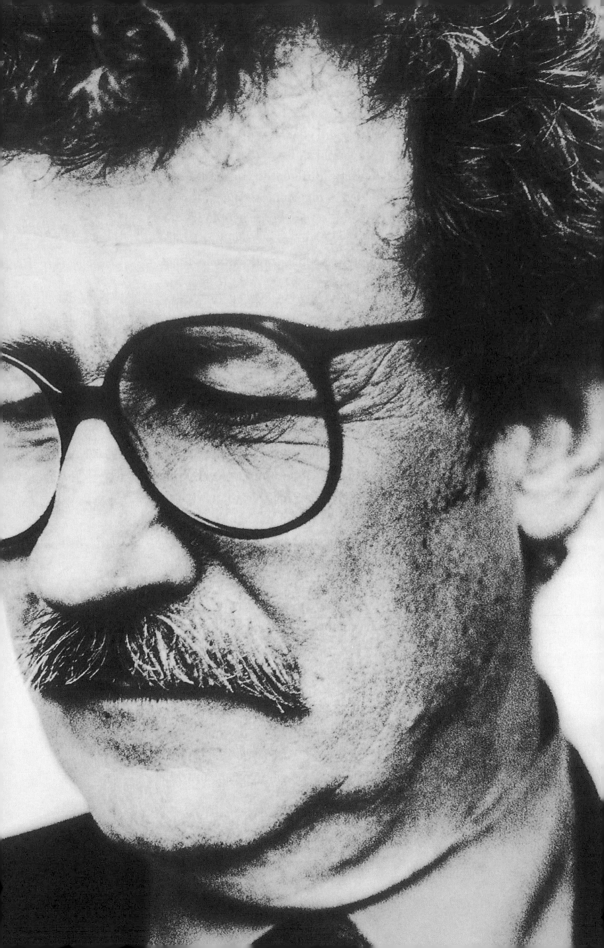

C hristopher Frayling is Rector of the Royal College of Art and Professor of Cultural History there. As a historian, critic and broadcaster he is well known for his work on radio and television. Acclaimed series include The Art of Persuasion *on Channel 4,* The Face of Tutankhamun *and* Strange Landscape – the illumination of the middle ages *on BBC2 and* Nightmare – the birth of horror *on BBC1. He has also had 13 books published on visual culture, design and history over the last 25 years. He is the longest serving Trustee of the V&A and the longest serving member of the Arts Council of England. In April 2000 he became chairman of the Design Council.*

Christopher Frayling

The genealogy of the concept *creative industries* is very interesting. It originates in the 1930s with a group of sociologists called The Frankfurt School who went to America from Germany and wrote about mass culture for the first time. They were appalled when they got there to find culture turning into an industry. They didn't like recordings, they liked live concerts. They didn't like the movies very much, they preferred live theatre. They hung on to high culture and saw its democratisation as a decline, an inevitable dumbing down. So for them coupling the word *industry* with the word *creative* was a pejorative, a link between a hard word and a soft one.

We then dissolve to 50 plus years later and the concept is back but its meaning has been reversed. I suspect that politicians, who were at university in the 1960s, read the phrase in their sociology textbooks and it stuck in their heads – and which has now become a label. It's now come to mean the opposite – a celebration of creative activities that contribute to the national economy.

What's very interesting is the fact that it still ghettoises creativity. It is based on the belief that there are certain professional activities where people are creative as a way of earning their living, rather than the thought that you have to sow creativity into every activity of life. It is patronising to others who are just as creative, but don't happen to belong to the club that owns the creative label and thinks it has a monopoly on creativity.

I feel strongly that it's very important to get away from this idea that unless you're a visualiser and happen to be in one of the visualising trades, you're not creative. I think that's extremely dangerous, and it smacks of 'styling'. I can understand why engineers and the manufacturing sector feel patronised by that. And now, suddenly, all the emphasis is on the virtual economy and creating the digital services of the future as if that alone equals creative. Even within the 'creative industries', services seemed to be getting all the publicity – the idea being that pure creativity and the virtual economy will come up with all the wonderful ideas that others will go off and produce. *'We'll write it, they'll print it'* is becoming an analysis of our economic future. But the people who 'print' are understandably feeling left out. Take someone like James Dyson, who is trying to have a one man industrial revolution in Malmsbury but feels totally circumvented by the debate because no one is talking about producing things any more.

There is a feeling within the relatively small world that I belong to, the visualising trades, that we've been treated too much in isolation over the last four or so years. Designers, artists and communicators have been able to enter a very supportive world. Their work has been praised to the skies, which is terrific. But that battle is won, and now the nurturing needs to be turned to other areas as well, areas that feel more out in the cold.

In the design world there's been a huge shift over the last few years from what you might call design with a big D to design with a little d. Design with a big D is the design professions: product design, graphic design, fashion design etc. We are Designers, and the word 'Design' has become the international way of describing us. Design with a little d is a much broader notion of design that encompasses the creative input and output that happens when you put design at the heart of business. That change in orientation and language has been going on over the last five or six years and so the notion of the Creative Industries is being left behind because it is too hung up on design with a big D.

This debate inevitably takes one into education and the importance of a creative, 'designerly' approach to all subjects rather than believing that you're only creative when you're in the art room. There is a slightly dangerous tendency to see the basic fundamental skills of the three Rs as being opposed to a more creative notion of education. It's becoming adversarial – the three Rs as the all important performance indicators, and the creative approach as liberal education theory of the 60s – when it should be integral.

There's been a huge expansion of creative subjects in higher education over the last 10–15 years. If you add together the total number of art and design graduates in the UK over a four-year period now, it is more than the population of Florence in the Renaissance. Now if they all expect a future in design with a big D, then we are over-producing to a huge extent, even though the creative professions are undoubtedly expanding. However, if they see it not as a vocational specialism, but as a very valuable thing to study for three years, providing them with a transferable and flexible set of skills, then the expansion is very exciting. When I studied history it was believed that the Humanities, like languages, were a good training for life – they developed powers of analysis and research and trained you to marshal a logical argument. We didn't expect to become professional historians or interpreters.

I know I'm biased, but I genuinely believe that a creative, design-based education could be hugely valuable in the future, where you're not going to be in one box for the whole of your life. You're going to chop and change. You're going to have to be flexible and nimble on your feet. You're going to have to write your own scenarios and work out ways of solving the problems you've set yourself. I think the designerly way of thinking could be extremely important to all of us and a great commercial resource but I don't think that either higher education or business has cottoned on to that yet.

At the Royal College of Art we don't believe that we're here to serve business, we believe that we're here to stimulate business. And business is desperate for stimulus. We want to produce people who can look at problems and challenges from many different angles and come up with stimulating new solutions or ideas that can have an economic impact. There's a feeling that the technology and infrastructure is miles ahead of the software and the ideas, which will be the engine that keeps them going. I've never known so many business people come to our summer shows hungry for new ideas – the oil to keep the engine going. It encourages me to believe that there is a real convergence of interest between creative education and business.

Typically a design graduate will leave the RCA now and set up a little business with three or four other people who are of their cohort, and offer the whole package. So instead of proclaiming themselves to the world as exclusively an industrial designer, they become part of a business with a graphic designer, an industrial designer, a thinker/writer, an architect and a fine artist and they present themselves to the world as being capable of firing on several cylinders. I think Pentagram, the design partnership, is probably the model for this on a large scale – they can do an interior, an installation, set up an event, do a graphic, design a product or finish a building. One of the biggest product designers in the country at the moment is the Norman Foster practice, doing contract furniture for his buildings. One of the RCA's recent ceramic graduates is now a hugely successful hat designer. Skills are seen as transferable and there is seamless movement around the design world. Whether this convergence is happening across business, and whether disciplinary boundaries are being challenged at a deep level, I find more difficult to tell.

The web is contributing to profound change. I don't mean designing web pages, which is a spin-off from graphics, but what happens – say – when somebody is able to design a car on the web from a kit provided by the Ford Motor Company? You customise your own product from a kit of parts. It has to happen sooner rather than later. Retail gone, showrooms gone, designers in the current sense, gone. The design community, especially established designers, is a bit uneasy and uncertain where it will fit in to all of this. And it's very generational; people in their 20s are excited and see this as a huge opportunity. People over 50, in my experience, can sometimes feel extremely threatened by it and have a tendency to retreat into an arts and crafts corner or to rail against progress. They feel like designosaurs.

Younger designers no longer feel defined by the skills base of a subject. They also realise that the business side of it – the management of projects and innovation – is as creative as the production of the product. This new concept of the mini-consortium is very exciting. In the 60s, 70s and 80s the great ambition was to set up on your own as a consultant. Before that the great ambition was to work in-house. Typically now, it's a team thing, much more collaborative and broadly based.

Art and design graduates seem able to create worlds around themselves. They are five times more likely to be self-employed than any other graduates. Take the company Deep End, run by Gary Lockwood. He was an industrial design engineer when he was at the RCA and within three years he had this huge company that deals with digital design. He didn't go to the business world and ask *'where can I find a slot?'*. He was flexibly minded and formed the world around himself. At the moment, that seems to be what's happening. People are asking *'why not?'*.

The graduates from the RCA go to wherever the action is. If a furniture designer thinks the action is in Barcelona, he or she will go and work in Barcelona. If a fashion designer thinks the action's in Tokyo, he or she will go and work in Tokyo. If a car designer thinks the action's in Germany, he or she will go and work in Germany. My job is to get them to the starting line.

They do sometimes feel that there is a greater culture of investing in fresh talent abroad. When someone's just left he or she may still be a bit rough at the edges, full of exciting ideas but not used to working within complex organisations or with teams. Traditionally British industry's been very frightened of such people, and will only invest in them a few years later when they've had the corners knocked off them. It's ironic because we have a strong reputation for mavericks and wildcards but seem unable to cope with the reality of them. Many of my graduates feel that they can develop overseas and make a name for themselves without being submerged in some corporate culture. Then typically they come back in their late 20s and set themselves up in business.

But they remain globetrotters and it is out of date to criticise that. A British design consultancy might make two-thirds of its money from Japan, Taiwan and Hong Kong. National chauvinism is not an issue for them. Maybe at this level there is a collision between the people working in the creative industries and the government's use of the idea of 'creative industry' as a boost to the British economy. It is shaky ground because for many of those involved, Britain is not their main market. Both 'D'esigners and 'd'esigners are citizens of the world.

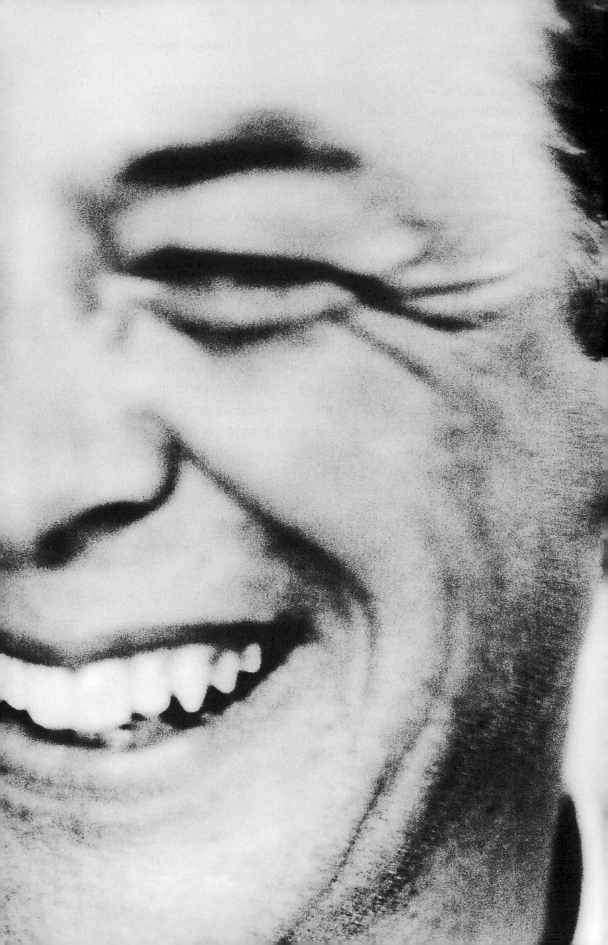

Rob Goffee is Professor of Organisational Behaviour at London Business School. He is also director of the Innovation Exchange at London Business School. He has held positions at a number of other universities – most recently at the Australian Graduate School of Management, University of New South Wales. He also acts as consultant to a number of major international companies. His research and publications are on the subjects of entrepreneurship, business formation and growth, corporate culture and managerial careers. He has published seven books including: Entrepreneurship in Europe; Women in Charge; Reluctant Managers *and, most recently,* The Character of a Corporation.

Rob Goffee

Tomorrow's winners in business will undoubtedly be those who can master the challenges of innovation and creativity on a continual basis. Competitive advantage will go to those who can invent the future. However, whilst we know a lot about what's stopped innovation; we know much less about what nurtures it and keeps it going.

It's difficult to predict an organisation's creativity and innovation by looking at the structure; what's much more likely to be predictive is the culture. The literature on innovation and creativity is very disappointing. It has tended to focus on R&D and 'big leap' innovation. There hasn't been a lot of work done on mapping behaviour and social relationships or on customer insights and how they correlate with innovation. There is no model for a large-scale innovative organisation so it would be difficult to tell you what one looked like.

In fact, typically, it is scale that inhibits innovation. Large-scale organisations are designed to repeat and persist, not necessarily to innovate and create. A lot of business practice is about organising repetition which can lead to incremental progress by doing the same thing better, more cheaply, more efficiently and with more productivity. You also tend to get two things in large-scale organisations: hierarchy and politics. There's fairly extensive evidence to show that excessive segmentation, and the political behaviour that goes with that, is antithetical to creativity.

There's no way we know of developing large-scale organisations without making them political and hierarchical. To get around this companies invent ways of re-creating smallness inside the organisation. One way is to allow different subcultures to emerge. Even those organisations to which we often attribute lots of innovation and creativity, such as 3M or Hewlett Packard, only have the looseness and flexibility that they are known for in relatively small parts. Large parts of those organisations are actually fairly conventional and hierarchical.

A key dimension in creative organisations is sociability. And sociability is a face-to-face construct. Sociability is linked with having fun. Fun is linked with being creative and innovative. The interesting thing about sociability is the question of how many people you can be sociable with. The evolutionary psychologists tell us it's about 150. Apparently the hunter gatherer tribes broke off a new tribe when they got to 150 because that was all they could handle. Yet in an era of rapidly growing companies and global business, the issue of sustaining face to face contact in a meaningful way becomes really difficult.

To make sense of company culture we need to understand the social relationships and structures operating within the organisation. There are two fundamental dimensions, sociability and solidarity, which I believe are predictive of certain kinds of behaviour and have something to do with creativity and innovation.

Sociability is a measure of natural friendliness between people. Friends help one another with no strings attached. The benefits to business are obvious – people enjoy working in friendly environments and they are more likely to be creative because sociability fosters teamwork, sharing information and being open to new ideas. It plays to an image of creativity which is about looseness, flexibility, space and slack in the system.

Solidarity, on the other hand, is based on a keen awareness of common goals and shared interests, whether people like each other or not. When these interests are threatened, high-solidarity organisations can mobilise their forces swiftly and ruthlessly. Solidarity inside an organisation is typically triggered by some notion of winning against someone else. Market pressure is a wonderful device for building solidarity. But the danger of organisations which have high solidarity, and therefore are very responsive to market signals – they have an enemy who they want to kill and a goal they want to achieve – is that they tend to be a little blinkered. If you imagine a high solidarity UK retail clearing bank, the mistake it would make is to focus only on other banks. We're NatWest, so we must kill Lloyds. We're Lloyds, so we must kill HSBC. They would miss the fact that the public wants to be able to cash a cheque in Waitrose. They would focus on the known enemy and so fail to anticipate the unknown enemy.

Fast change creates a lot of pressure towards greater solidarity because, unless you react, you're out of business. These days it's getting faster and faster and you've got to react quicker and quicker. If you've got to react quickly, you need solidarity. In the 90s many companies aimed at a high solidarity ideal because a shared vision and commitment to common goals could be seen to drive growth. But the danger is that people only co-operate when individual advantage is clear and if the overall strategic focus of the organisation is wrong, they will commit suicide very quickly.

Mars is a *high solidarity* organisation and Unilever is a *high sociability* organisation, so the ice cream wars they engaged in are a good illustration of how they behave. Some years ago when someone at Mars thought up the idea of turning confectionery into ice cream, they were fantastically effective – quick application, fast to market. They were attacking, amongst others, Unilever, because Unilever owned Wall's. When Mars introduced their ice cream, it appeared that they had the biggest ice cream manufacturer on the back foot in some European markets. But now, if you walk into your garage forecourt, you will often see Magnum, and Magnum is made by Wall's. They did fight back, but, because they believe strategies are about a long game, they fought back by building long-term relationships.

Unilever has got a great business in Brazil because, when times got tough, they stayed around and they've been there for over 30 years. Procter & Gamble, a high solidarity competitor, is more prone to move in and out at speed according to more short term results.

High sociability, low solidarity organisations are better at tolerating diversity. Because if you think about it, low solidarity is saying it's OK to be different. Diversity is definitely correlated with creativity. That's the good news. The bad news is that diversity is more difficult to manage. When Unilever buys a company like Calvin Klein Cosmetics in New York, it will allow them the space to operate in their own way because it accepts that they know the market best and they know the action in New York. The problem with organisations which are high solidarity and don't allow enough diversity, is that they make acquisitions and try to convert them.

Unilever has just bought Ben & Jerry's. The great challenge is to allow Ben and Jerry to carry on being Ben & Jerry. The evidence is that they will. They are continuing to pay a proportion of profits to environmental causes, and Ben and Jerry are being kept as consultants. It's the kind of give and take you'd expect from a high sociability, low solidarity company.

A high sociability organisation accepts that relationships are complicated and that therefore the interface between what you do and what I do can never be fully nailed down contractually. There's an unarticulated reciprocity. You need that, particularly in knowledge based economies, to encourage people to share their insights, wisdom, information and data. If you've got an organisation where people want to give things away, then it is probably going to be better at creativity. Accumulating knowledge is not the point; the point is to apply it and use it creatively. To do that in organisations, you've got to move it around. If you don't move it around, you're not using it.

The American style is to tie a business relationship down via a contract as tightly and as specifically as possible. They do a deal and that tends to result in short or medium-term exchanges which work for a while. The Asian or Japanese approach is completely opposite. They would build trust first, and once they'd talked to each other to see if they could work together, then they'd get on to the business. What you typically get are longer-term collaborations which can produce different sorts of innovation.

The innovation process is different in different cultures and sectors. The application of creativity in complex manufacturing systems involves disciplined attention to detail and systems. As a nation Britain does not always seem to have the necessary patience for this. Our car industry was decimated in the 1960s and 1970s, because we faced Japanese and German competitors who knew what quality was. Quality in the car industry, as in other manufacturing industries, is about careful, incremental application of good ideas. The Japanese and the Germans have taught us how to do that in the car industry, so we're not innately unsuited to it, but we've had to do it under their auspices.

If you then think about the process of creative application in, say, advertising or mobile phones, it is quite different. Take Orange, a great UK success story in the 1990s – where did its success come from? Was it the brilliant manufacture of mobile phones? No, because anybody can make them or the systems that support them. Their success came from creative brand development rather than technology.

The creative challenge for the dot.com economy is how to manage growth of a speed and pace none of us, up until now, have been familiar with. It's difficult enough to manage growth full stop. One vision is that all you do is manage it for four or five years, then you sell up and get rich, which was the end game.

But I heard someone say that the people who are going into dot.com companies to make money will not be the winners. It is the people that are going into dot.com companies to change the world who will win. And I think that's true. People worth billions, like Bill Gates, carry on because they're driven by something else. So the ones worth putting your money into are the ones led by people who want to change the world.

What dot.com shows in absolute polarity is something you see elsewhere but often in less extreme form. You see people who just want to get by; they don't want to change the world, they just want to become let's say, a partner in their accounting firm. They neither want to change the world nor earn buckets of money, they're just happily scooting along. The dot.com companies, and the mythology surrounding them, is having a destabilising effect on everyone else. People who once thought they were doing rather well, now realise they aren't, or at least think they aren't. Dissatisfaction is beginning to take hold. Dissatisfied people find it difficult to be creative.

Many corporate people are battle weary. If you've worked in a big organisation for the last 10 or 20 years and you've survived, you've almost certainly suffered pain, recession, cutbacks, re-engineering, 27 change programmes and three different leaders preaching different songs. Tired battle weary people will not be creative, and to go into those companies and say, *'be creative and have some fun'* is almost an insult. There are many work places now that don't feel like much fun and you won't change them overnight. There is nothing worse than clever, political people who feel miserable.

It is a difficult balance because there is a tough side to creative organisations. You need people to be stretched and motivated and not to be too comfortable, but if they're overstretched and have no time for co-operation, then the danger is they won't deliver innovation at all. Some stretch and discipline is needed but also support and scope for growth. Innovative organisations are driven by high internal standards; they have a certain edge that keeps them alert.

Hermann Hauser has extensive experience of developing and financing companies in the information technology sector. Since 1986 he has founded over 20 new technology companies. In 1997 Amadeus Capital Partners was created to establish a venture capital fund to invest in early stage UK based technology companies with global potential. It is based in London and Cambridge.

Hermann Hauser was born and educated in Vienna. He came to Cambridge in 1977 to complete a PhD in Physics and has maintained close research links with the University since.

He co-founded Acorn Computer Group in 1978 and in 1986 became vice president of research at Olivetti where he established a global network of research laboratories.

In 1984 he was voted computer personality of the year in Britain and in 1999 he was made an Honorary fellow of King's College, Cambridge.

Hermann Hauser

There is a certain Darwinian aspect to creativity. You start with an undergrowth of ideas that go through a 'creative' filter and the filtrate is those ideas that succeed. It is heavily dependent on an environment where new ideas can be fostered and succeed. The premier environment for high-tech companies is undoubtedly Silicon Valley. It is very creative – many different new business models, new ideas and processes are being tried out there. Some of them succeed, most of them don't, but you end up with some different ways of doing things that have stood the test of time. When it comes to venture capital, Silicon Valley is the place where this evolutionary process has had more time to come up with good, new solutions than anywhere else in the world.

There are lots of different ways in which you can do venture capital. Creating an avalanche of value is not always what's needed. The world is not a stable place and you may need to change things around and get different partners in. For that reason our fund is based on a 10-year partnership, an idea that came from Silicon Valley and reflects the dynamic nature of venture capital.

Silicon Valley is very experimental, something which I think is driven by its immigrant culture. It's the American Dream at work. The old story holds true – if somebody drives a Ferrari in Silicon Valley, everybody says, *'Wow, what a car, I'm going to have one of those in a few years time'.* If somebody drives a Ferrari here, others scratch it because they have no belief that they could ever own one themselves.

The culture is transferable and it is becoming instilled in Cambridge via an options system. Until two or three years ago, options were simply viewed as a way to get base salaries down, and so very little value was attached to them. This had a lot to do with the British attitude to money. If you ask people here how they could get a lot of money, the answer is by stealing. There are some exceptions; they might have inherited it, in which case their forefathers stole it. This has now changed dramatically. If you look at the *Sunday Times* 1000 Rich List, you'll find that no fewer than 75% of the richest 1000 people in this country are self-made. This is in large part due to options. They are resulting in academics and high quality corporate managers being willing to join start-ups. Take two of Amadeus's companies – ARM is now worth $11 billion and has made 200 millionaires; Virata is worth $2.5 billion and has made over 100 millionaires. These options have real value.

The ability to make money does fuel the process but ultimately there is little that money can buy you. It's not that useful since there's only so much you can eat during the day and there are only so many Ferraris that you can buy. One of the nice things about high-technology and one of the reasons why it's such a fly-wheel, is that those people that make money in high-technology immediately reinvest it in high-technology. What's happening is really quite exciting. If you take just three Cambridge companies – ARM, Virata and Autonomy, they account for £1.5 billion in share options – that's £1.5 billion going into Cambridge to foster the hi-tech sector. It's not a government scheme, and it's not an endowment or an investment by a pension fund; it's hundreds of individual people putting in their own money. They are what we call 'business angels'– essentially someone who has enough money to provide seed funding. And that is the unsung story of Silicon Valley. Everybody knows about the successes of venture capital companies in Silicon Valley, but business angels invest four times more than venture capitalists. So the real money that drives success in Silicon Valley comes from the business angels, not the venture capitalists.

I started as an entrepreneur, then I built about 25 companies as a serial entrepreneur and then I became a business angel because I was known as a sucker for technology. I would give money where most people wouldn't. Over the past 10 years or so, I've probably provided around half of the 'angel money' in

Cambridge because I was one of the first people who made some money in the Cambridge area. We're talking small amounts – £10 million or so – compared with the £1.5 billion out there now. Business angels are spending their money helping other people fulfil their ideas and grow their companies. The real creativity, in my view, is found in this network of people who have a genuine interest and take real enjoyment in what they are doing with their money. It has a lot to do with lifestyle; it gives me a great buzz to help young people start companies. The money, as it turns out, is only a small part of it. The main value of the business angel is that they've been through it all before. This experience is what enables them to mentor.

I look for five things when I'm thinking of putting money in a business. The first is whether or not there is a real need for whatever they're proposing. That's hard to instil. I tell them rather crudely, *'Take the toilet as number 10, something you really need and need every day. Now try to get as far as number 1'.* It's hard to find something people really need because we don't actually need a lot. Sometimes new ideas spin out from existing companies that already have a business model and where they know that there is a market. And sometimes it's the reverse, especially on the internet, where you say, *'OK we can now do things differently, so let's find a market where we can really make a difference'.*

So criteria 1 is the need. Number 2 is the size and the growth rate of the market. Number 3 is the quality of the team – have they done it before? are they credible? are they backable? Sadly, for a propeller head like myself, the technology only comes in at Number 4. Number 5 is the ability to do partnership deals.

With the technology it is usually know-how; only rarely is it breakthrough innovation which you can patent. But even know-how that gets you 6 to 12 months ahead of the competition can be invaluable. You can build a company around that.

But if there is a choice between an A team with C technology and a C team with A technology, sadly the A team with C technology wins every time. The quality of the team is more important than the quality of the technology.

The way we think about the team is that it needs at least one creative star. Around the Cambridge area it is often the technology star that we back. But if we can find a marketing or operations star we'll build them in. Stars have this electrifying effect on the team because they're head and shoulders above anybody else in the industry. They inspire loyalty, and a belief that ordinary work is just not good enough. A small company needs to pull together and needs an attitude of, *'Right, we're going to show them'*. You get creativity by providing an environment in which people can be creative, and that's normally associated with small teams and very strong leadership from people who've got a vision that they're willing to articulate and can get a team of people to sign up to.

That attitude used to be more American than British. But one of the most satisfying things I've been involved with in the past 10 years was launching the Business Plan competition at Cambridge University. We had 400 undergraduates in a lecture hall and the spirit was, *'We're just as smart and hard working as these guys from Stanford and MIT, we'll just show them all what we can do'.* It was run by the Cambridge Entrepreneurship Society, which is a student body that cuts across all departments. It was entirely organised by the students. There was great enthusiasm for it and the winners won £50,000 and an invitation, all expenses paid, to Stanford for the International Business Plans competition. There's now an international network, a kind of 'club' of enterprising, likeminded people out there. It's very exciting.

There is enthusiasm for business but it's for starting businesses or joining early stage companies and not large corporations. There is an increasing divide between large and small companies and when it comes to bridging the gap, large British corporations are amongst the worst offenders in the world. Large American companies have learnt, mainly through corporate venturing arms, how to interface with small companies. They invest in small companies and at least a part of the large company speaks the language of small companies. The interplay of the small creative companies with the large corporations has contributed to the Silicon Valley success.

Cisco is probably the best example; they have the highest market capitalisation in the world and this success is entirely built on a brilliantly executed strategy of acquiring small innovative companies. They have a *'Cisco way'*, aimed particularly at those things small companies are notoriously bad at, like accounting procedures. But they retain a lot of the creative talent by giving them sufficient room to take advantage of the infrastructure, the phenomenal brand and phenomenal sales channels in order to commercially exploit their innovations. So small teams dream up new ideas and then they've got this fantastic support from a huge company which does the manufacturing, the quality control, the selling and the aftersales service.

At the opposite end of the spectrum you get the typical British acquisition policy where the merger or acquisition is mainly a defensive, tactical move to maximise short-term return rather than to build new businesses and expand.

I believe companies have an interesting attribute which I call their genes. These genes get moulded or created during the very early phases of the company and they seem to stay with the company for evermore. It can be difficult to fight the genes of a large corporation that has operated in a certain way for a long time. Conversely a company where being lean, mean and creative and doing things differently was part of its intrinsic emotional and intellectual set up, will want to prove itself every quarter. Those genes come from the founders and will stay with it. Apple is probably the best and one of the most extreme examples of this.

Britain has the right cultural genes because we started the industrial revolution. We are not a lost cause although we may have to rediscover, train and exercise these genes. I think that creativity in business depends a lot on the quality of the entrepreneur and on their leadership skills. British entrepreneurs are still quite amateurish but I feel a lot of the basic skills can be taught. That's why I set up the Entrepreneurship Centre in Cambridge. We need more centres like this around the country and we need it to start in schools. Entrepreneurs should be role models and starting a business should be something school children dream of doing. Large companies also need to be taught to be more entrepreneurial themselves. Reuters is a prime example that should be followed. They had an outstanding corporate venturing arm that is now being floated off as The Greenhouse Fund. So there are some who are doing it, although they remain some way behind their American colleagues.

P atricia Hewitt is the Labour MP for Leicester West and Minister for Small Business and E-commerce. Her previous ministerial post was as Economic Secretary at the Treasury.

In the 1980s Patricia Hewitt was Press and Publicity Officer and later Policy Co-ordinator for the then Leader of the Opposition, Neil Kinnock. She then became Deputy Director of the Institute for Public Policy Research followed by three years as Director of Research at Andersen Consulting.

Patricia Hewitt was born and educated in Australia. She is married and has two teenage children.

Patricia Hewitt

I 'd like to start by talking about the textile industry since I'm also the Textiles Minister. Textiles is seen, quite wrongly, as an old industry in terminal decline. For all those firms that are competing at the low value end of the market and who will probably not survive long against foreign competition, there are as many firms that are hi-tech, high value added and highly creative. I visited one recently called Textured Jersey which is in my constituency. They've created a modern working environment in a 19th-century mill. Part of the factory actually looks like a science or pharmaceuticals lab. They're taking colour and playing with the chemistry of dyeing and the impact of different kinds of dyes on different kinds of materials and they are creating new high performance textiles. There is huge investment in R&D and they are a global leader. It's a highly creative business and it's organised in a way that seems to me to be a common thread in creative organisations – putting people together in ways that enable new ideas to be thought through and then acted upon. At Textured Jersey the creative and commercial people all sit together in an open plan office sharing space and ideas, and right next door to them is the research laboratory and the new machinery where they can put those ideas into practice.

They are being creative all the way through the value chain. It's one thing to create new products from existing technology but a very innovative company can also create a whole new technology. At Textured Jersey the ideas don't just come from the R&D scientists; they might equally come from the people who are close to the customers' needs, the machine suppliers, the machine buyers or the factory floor people who are actually operating the machinery. What you have, effectively, is a constant conversation along the lines of, *wouldn't it be more exciting if we could do this? Now hang on, if we want to do that we'll need machinery that can do this. And what if we pleated this textile and can we get wavy pleats?'* 'What ifs' are constantly being asked.

But levels of creativity vary drastically from firm to firm, even within the same sector. One of our big, successful clothing retailers told me about a recent experience with a textile manufacturer. The retailer explained that they often needed fast, short runs because market demand changes so quickly. They needed to know if the manufacturer could provide this level of flexibility. When the manufacturer told them how many weeks it would take to turn round an order of that kind the retailer asked how many part-timers they employed. The answer was *'four out of four hundred'*. The retailer then asked if they could take on some more part timers to stretch the shifts and do what was required. The manufacturer's reply was *'Oh God, no. If we offer people part-time work, they'll all want it'*.

There was a management that wasn't willing to do what the customer wanted and wasn't willing to offer the working hours that the employees wanted. The chances of that firm surviving, are, I would say, very slim. It's simply not a creative company.

I'm a great believer in the importance of diversity and co-location. By that I mean putting people from different disciplines together. It applies in the think-tank world, which needs to be a creative environment. It's using brainstorming as a more or less permanent process. When I was at the IPPR, we were constantly bringing together people from different disciplines to work in teams on particular sets of issues and that was the foundation of our creative thinking. A seminar we held on family policy was an interesting case in point. We brought together people from family policy with people from family therapy and child developmental psychology. We assumed that they would all know each other and we would be the newcomers, but instead we were the common element. Most of these people had never spoken to each other before and out of the discussion came a highly distinctive view of family policy.

Natural communication and sharing of information does

inevitably slow down with size. When we started the IPPR there were three people in one room in a serviced office but it quickly got to the point where we needed more space so that we were no longer bumping into each other. However, being spread across two floors inhibited communication, so we then had to begin to organise for it.

I also spent a couple of years with Andersen Consulting, which of course is huge. When I was there it had 35,000 people in 55 countries, and now it's much bigger. If you're operating in 55 countries and you're in every sector of the economy, you know a huge amount. Small units can be creative and agile but scale gives you the power of knowledge. The trick is to make both these elements work for you. Whilst I was there Andersen installed one of the world's largest intranets. Digital networks enable knowledge management – you can codify information and use intelligent agents to find things out with much greater efficiency and it can reach out and include far more people.

Using high technology to better effect does not necessarily require us to look to America. I think that firms are finding their own way. Cambridge Electronics is a good example. They gave up the lease on their building and decided to make themselves a virtual organisation. Everybody works wherever they want, they're all on laptops and working on the web. But because they weren't sure it would work, they put their furniture in store. A year later they sold the furniture because it was such a phenomenal success. They have a secure website for every client and their workings are totally transparent so Cambridge Electronics effectively becomes part of the client organisation they are working with. The interesting part is that most of their clients, leading-edge firms on the West Coast of the USA, were genuinely surprised by the service they received from this UK-based firm.

Another advantage of networks is that they can enable shared group work. One of the big aircraft manufacturers designed an aircraft wing, a hugely complex process, using a team of engineers and designers across three time zones and in multiple locations. It was developed virtually and that slashes the cost. Information and Communication technology (ICT) allows you to create a prototype before you've put a single screw into a piece of metal.

My impression is that large-scale engineering operations are about creative teams rather than individual creativity. I do think it's a mistake to see creativity as purely individual. Most of us have, at some level, a whole strand of personal creativity that will show itself in different ways, but most of us are also capable of operating effectively as part of a creative team. There is plenty of evidence to suggest that you can get much more powerful results from a team than you can get from any one of those individuals working separately.

I heard one of our leading biologists talking about what is happening in the human genome field which involves massive datasets held in different parts of the world. Science does tend to proceed through extraordinary breakthroughs which are ul-timately about individual creativity. What is interesting, however, is that this is enabled by the collective process of making the data, and interpretations of the data, available to everybody instantly through the wonders of ICT. So it's neither purely individual nor purely collective, it's a bit of both.

That's why the term 'the new economy' is problematic. It implies that traditional manufacturing – engineering, cars, tex-tiles – are the old economy and it's just a matter of time before they die. But that fails to recognise how technology has the power to transform every production process and every product within every sector at every turn. In successful firms creativity is everywhere.

The job creation rate in this country is going up very fast and those jobs are not being created in sleepy, bureaucratic organisations that are committed to business as usual. They're developing in lots of different sectors and they are being created in companies that are either doing new things or doing old things in new ways. The whole cycle of job and business creation and destruction has speeded up. Take the financial sector – lots of take-overs and job losses but also great regeneration as the sector transforms itself. It's not like the destruction of the coal mines where people had nowhere else to go and whole communities were destroyed. Financial services are alive and well and employing an awful lot of people – they have not been left on the scrap heap.

If you take an example like First Direct, I also think business creativity comes from being passionate about what you are doing and how you do it. And if we believe that people, knowledge and creativity are the real economic assets in the modern world, then the natural ownership form is employee ownership. If the people – both individually and in teams – create the value, then they've got to own the value. If they don't own it, either they'll stop creating the value because the edge won't be there, or else they'll set up their own company or go to a company where they can be a co-owner.

Amazon are trebling their warehouse space in Milton Keynes so I asked them what their starting rate was for a packer in the warehouse. It's £6 an hour *and* share options because, they explained, they want everybody in the firm to think like owners. They find it makes people willing to go that extra mile.

Share options are becoming a given, particularly in IT and dot.com start-ups but also increasingly in established firms. This new alignment of interests is a million miles away from the old, built-in conflict between owners and managers and workers of the past.

Business start-ups are becoming very popular and City institutions and management consultants are struggling to get people and keep them because once they get the training and some experience, they may well move out to a start-up. Several large institutions are setting up incubators in-house and spinning off their own start-ups which they keep within the 'family' in order to retain their best people.

I was a child of the 1960s and I came from the world of radical student activism. Now that young radicalism is in leading-edge business. And you see some of the bigger, established businesses who, ten years ago, would have sneered at these upstarts throwing off their suits and ties in order to partner them or be like them.

I would like my own children to be exposed to some of the exciting creativity going on in business right now and to have some first-hand experience of it. I've been in public service most of my career and my husband is a lawyer, so we provide a very traditional British middle-class model. I would like them to be aware of other possibilities.

There is still a disturbing old British trait which involves turning up one's nose at trade. This anti-commercial snobbery has held us back over the last two centuries. People who say business can't be creative because it's all commercial don't know what modern business is about. They've probably never even been inside a leading-edge creative company, whether it's engineering, textiles, graphic design or IT. These are all now hugely exciting places to be.

Michael Jackson

Michael Jackson established Elderstreet in 1990 and is currently Executive Chairman. He is a specialist in raising finance and investing in the smaller companies sector. Elderstreet currently manages £140 million of funds. In 1983 Michael became an investor in, and director of, The Sage Group, the leading supplier of accounting and payroll software. Since then its capitalisation has risen from £1 million to over £9 billion. He is currently its Chairman. He is also a director of several other quoted and unquoted companies.

The single most important thing in business is having a very high energy level. You've got this mass of stuff coming at you and a timeframe that doesn't allow you the time not to make decisions. So I'm not sure it's creativity, I think it's just trying to stay one step ahead of the game the whole time. It's about being constantly on the ball, shaking things up, keeping the momentum going. You need to let people know that you're on their back, you're always niggling away, it's almost like having a nasty little pin pricking across many different fronts. There's both fear and greed at the bottom of it – greed that if you don't do this deal, someone else is going to do it and they're going to make a killing. And fear that you could do it and it could go wrong. It's highly charged stuff.

I think I'm more genuinely creative on the boards of other companies. It's much better to go into situations from the outside. I've made some horrendous mistakes because I've been too close and it's all become too complex. Whereas when I go on to other people's boards I can often see very clearly what they should be doing.

I do believe the key to success is someone taking the lead and not being frightened to make a real decision and go for it. It's often about gut instinct – really believing in things and sticking your neck out. You've got to go for it, and accept that you have to change as you go for it – there are times that you have to go fast, and times you have to go slow. Watch good tennis players – they change their tactics often. They'll stop serving and volleying, or slow the game down with a lob, or change the angle of attack from the forehand to the backhand – subtle changes which you'll only recognise if you're a very good tennis player, and which can make a massive difference to the outcome of the match. That ability to know when to change the angle of attack and when to change the momentum of the game is the difference between a No. 1 player, a top 20 player and a top 100 player. Now is that creativity? I think it is – an element of fine tuning and change which makes the difference between someone that wins the game and someone who doesn't. And I think that's equally true of what we do; when is the right time to go for it? when is the right time to hold back? when is the right time to go out and hire the most expensive people you can? It's very fluid, but like a tennis game, those are some of the things which make the difference.

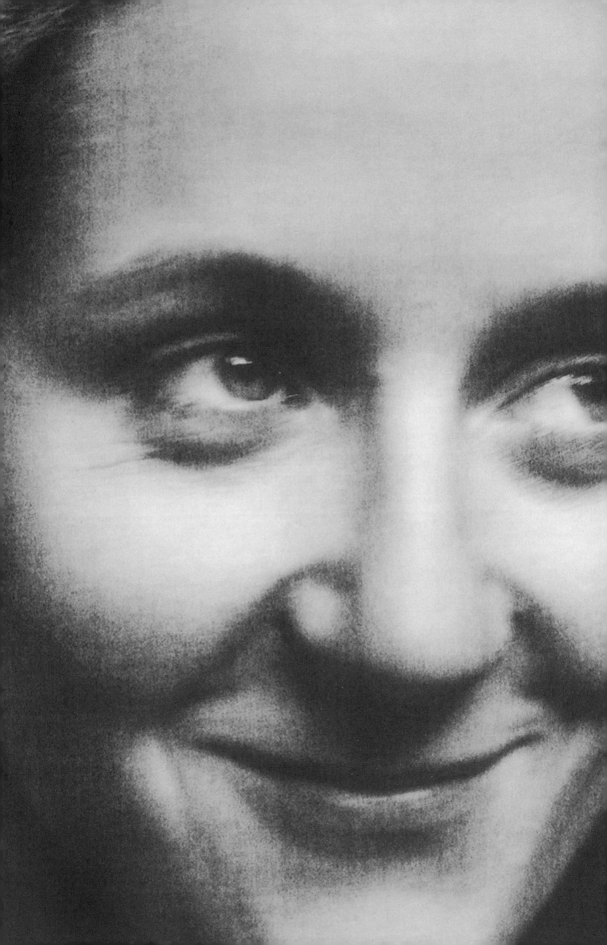

Martha Lane Fox, 27, is co-founder and Chief Operating Officer of lastminute.com, the on-line retailer, which she and Brent Hoberman launched in April 1998. Last-minute.com aims to match late availability from service providers such as airlines, hotels, car rental, tour operators and ticket agencies with the public's desire for a bargain. On its stockmarket flotation in March 2000, lastminute.com had 1.4 million subscribers, employed 250 people and was the second best known e-commerce brand in Britain. Martha began her career at Spectrum Strategy Consultants where she specialised in pay TV and then moved to Carlton where she was head of network development.

Martha Lane Fox

I t's practically two years to the day since Brent and I raised the first amount of money. I certainly feel we've had to be creative in establishing ourselves, building credibility and breaking down barriers. Every time someone's thrown up a wall we've needed to be creative to think our way around it. Luckily we're both dogged and tenacious.

Just believing in something and wanting to make it happen is very powerful. If you believe there is a route forward it motivates you to try. Getting a good idea off the ground and proving people wrong means that you're forced into creative thinking. You need to bash down those four walls. At the beginning I was trying to get the right people within airlines, hotel chains and entertainment companies to pay attention to what was basically two nutters with a business plan. We had no website we could show them; we just had to get them to believe that what we were babbling on about was something that we could really deliver. This meant small things like chatting up secretaries, getting mobile numbers, learning about where a person might be week on week and where you could catch them. The trick was not to give up after you'd tried calling them 10 times, when they're never in the office, but to say OK, they're never in the office, but they will be at this big airline conference so I'll wait outside and corner them there. We never lied but maybe we inflated the stage of development that we were at. Instead of saying we had an idea for a website, we said we were about to launch a website. It is critical not to believe that the situation you're in is going to last forever.

One of the only things I don't think we've done wrong, is to aim very high and move very fast. We got Peter Bouw, who had run KLM, to be our Chairman before we'd even launched our website. We thought we could be pan-European within a year and we were. You just set goals that seem absolutely outrageous and then you will probably end up half way towards them. By setting huge standards you lift the mood up. If you ask anyone here, they'd say, *'Yeah we're going to be global, we're going to be a huge player'*. It doesn't really matter whether we do that in 6 months, 5 years or 10 years, it's the fact that everyone knows we're trying to be number one and the best. Ambition is crucial. When I initially sought advice, several people suggested raising about £100,000 and doing it in a small way to see what happened. It was completely the wrong advice; if you're going to do it, you have to do it big. Basically the web is about scale, it's about being global, it's about being able to exploit synergies across business, to justify technology cost and to justify people cost, and to do that you do need to aim large.

We're a strange phenomenon now – a start-up plc. We're well known, so we're big in some ways but we're absolutely minuscule in other ways. I think that we're quite humble as a company. We appreciate that this is a high-risk idea with a big vision and we've still got a huge amount to do. So the creative thinking becomes about how to make the company one stage bigger all the time in order to get one step nearer profitability. The creativity doesn't go after the start-up because in the grand scheme of things we're nowhere near where we want to be. Now the challenge is how to catapult the business into another league of size, scale and success. As a start-up you have no history or baggage, and that allows you to be more objective and to move with lightning speed into lots of different areas.

We have four open planned floors and 300 staff. Even if we can't – as we could even just six months ago – include every-body in all the decisions, you can have small groups that are em-powered to do things. For example, we have this group called the Jedi Council which is ten of the brightest people in the company regardless of which part of the company they've come from, who are trying to think about where we should be in one year's time. They report directly to Brent and I and come up with fresh thinking across the whole business.

Similarly, we have a social committee, which again is ten

people from across the business, who are trying to think about ways of keeping the office a nice place to be and ensuring that everyone feels that they're plugged into a network of other people.

We've recruited nearly 300 people in 18 months. The company changes so fast that it requires different kinds of people every month. We need people who are inherently quite young in their attitudes and who are not threatened by the speed of change. You can't stand still, you can't be crippled by not knowing what the right answer is; you just have to make a decision. We make 100 decisions every day, ten of which will be right and move the business forward. But you do need to bring very experienced people on board and our top management team are from Club Med, IBM and KLM. Brent and I also need to constantly question whether we're the right people to be doing the roles that we are doing.

This is an extraordinary environment and people come into it with their eyes open. The hours are longer, the pressure is greater and you have more responsibility. You need to be nimble and quick to embrace change and see how it affects you. We're constantly asking people here to reassess what they're good at. Practically everyone's had to change role, take a step down or take a step up. In other companies there's a lot more ego and a mindset, which says, *'this is my area of responsibility and this is what I do'*. Everyone here would have sunk ages ago if they'd had that kind of attitude. People need to come into this place with a little bit of an entrepreneurial spirit, or at least respecting those who are like that; otherwise I think we lose something as a company. You have to like the concept and you have to be committed – it just doesn't work otherwise.

It is also a very difficult environment. There is a trade off in terms of structure and process, although we do understand that people need to know where they're sitting, what they're doing and where they're going. But there's nothing like the structure and support that you'd get in a normal company of this size.

Having said that I've never worked in an environment where people are so loyal and committed. I don't expect many people that are here now to be here in five years' time, but that doesn't mean that you're not loyal to the company or that you don't have enormous commitment while you're here. Time-frames and expectations have shifted and the intensity of the working environment has changed dramatically. Creative ways of employing and motivating people are very important. Fitting slightly square pegs into round holes in this kind of environment can be really good. It can be more chaotic, but it can also produce good results. And of course every single person here has quite significant share options. That culture of ownership really makes a difference.

In business terms what we are doing is not fundamentally different. It relies on a genuine market, a very solid business model and a competitive advantage. Deep down our business is about providing great products and services to customers and the core of what we do is technology, supplier relations and customer care and service. That's the nuts and bolts of our business. What we're doing is providing a supplier outlet for products at the last minute – we're matching buyers and sellers at short notice. To date there has never been any way to get the best yield at the last minute because of the speed and scale it requires. We've found a way of facilitating this exchange via the immediacy of the net.

The web is extraordinary and does change aspects of the business model. It allows suppliers and customers to talk to each other in different ways. It lowers pricing because it is more transparent, so people can undercut each other and cut their distribution costs by changing distribution channels. It offers new levels of choice and convenience. You can go on to a website and select all airlines, look at all the prices and all the fare classes at the click of a button. That is something you could never do before unless you were a travel agent. It empowers the customer in an exciting, new way. And that's just in business, let alone the impact on health or education, or the ability for people to communicate from the far reaches of the world. All of which I find immensely exciting.

I think there is a huge misconception about dot.com companies. Success will show that, as with traditional business, it's all about creating products that people want and which will prove useful to them. The market will shake out those people who believe that dot.com commerce is about buying domain names and heavy marketing because that's not what it's about, and ultimately I don't believe that they will be successful.

The ones that will be successful are the ones doing something that is enabled by the new technology, rather than just taking something from the off-line world and putting it on-line. It's also about being the prime mover because, as we've seen in the US, brand is everything. Look at Amazon, which built a phenomenal brand and can now sell people anything on the back of it. It's about global potential and huge market opportunities like priceline.com in the US where you can roll out into hundreds of new categories. I think there are characteristics by which you can judge the wheat from the chaff.

Lastminute.com is not a travel agency or a bucket shop on line. It should be a site you use every day because it should answer your needs, whether it's, *'I've got to get a babysitter'* or, *'I need to fly away'* or, *'I've forgotten someone's birthday'* or, *'I want to book a restaurant'* or, *'I want to book the cinema'*, or, *'What's on TV tonight?'* Every last minute decision that you make, we want to have the content there to help you make it.

To do this we knew that we had to build a brand very, very, fast. We've spent a fraction of what other dot.com companies have on advertising. We did talk to the press, although we never anticipated that there would be so much personality based interest in us. We always felt we wanted people to be able to see the faces behind the company, and for it not to be just another faceless product or service. We didn't want it to be *our* faces — that's just how it turned out. There's no doubt the PR and the awareness has come from people's interest in us. It totally overwhelmed me but I think that it occurred because we were one of the first start-ups to come out of Europe that was not just a copy of a US idea and yet behaved like a US-style company. The name is also so infectious — lastminute.com — it tells you what we do and I think that was hugely helpful in getting people to recognise it.

The attitude of the press in this country, particularly seen from the outside, has been extraordinary. The unbelievable way in which you're built up only to be knocked down, and the sudden about turns with no editorial control. It was all so frenetic and haywire. US investors were genuinely amazed and a couple of our board members, who come from the US, simply could not understand the phenomenal situation that we found ourselves in. In the US the attitude is much more relaxed; it's a question of, *'look what you're trying to do — maybe it'll work, maybe it won't, but well done for having a go'*. There is less fear of failure and a more positive attitude towards people trying to do it on their own. It's fine to have had ten businesses all go belly-up; it shows you're prepared to take a risk. We have two people working in senior management here who had businesses that went bankrupt. We thought that was a bonus but the papers criticised us for employing irresponsible managers.

I've learnt a lot from things I've done badly — like a bad university degree and the mistakes we've made in this business. It's important to have the confidence to take the knocks, to understand that failure isn't a disaster and that your life doesn't have to follow some pre-ordained course. In that sense I think the market correction we've just experienced as a business is probably a good thing for the long term.

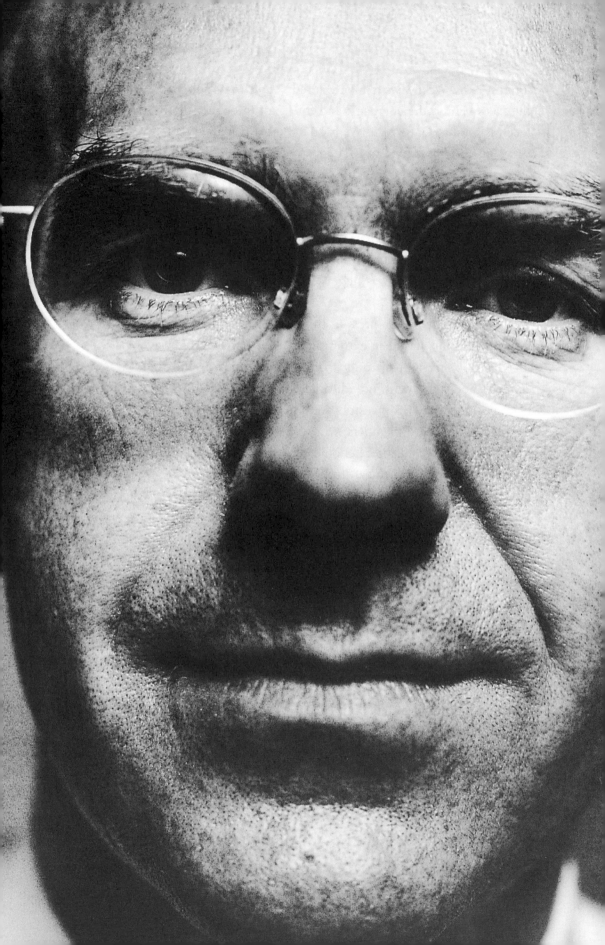

Terry Leahy

Terry Leahy was appointed Chief Executive of Tesco, Britain's leading food retailer, in March 1997. Tesco's share of the British retail market has increased throughout the 1990s and currently stands at 15.5%. Annual sales exceed £20 billion and the company employs 200,000 people in the UK alone. Its internet grocery business is the largest in the world and its non-food business is growing rapidly. The company now has operations throughout Europe and in Asia and in three out of the past four years Tesco has been voted Britain's most admired company. Terry Leahy joined Tesco in 1979 as a marketing executive. His focus has always been customer driven, from 1984–1988 he held the position of Marketing Director for Tesco Stores Ltd and then in 1992 he joined the board of Tesco plc with responsibility for marketing.

Many people do regard Tesco as being innovative. That makes you stand back and take a fresh look at your own business, what it does and what it has done, and ask yourself what it is they see in the business that they call innovation. I think it's about a number of interesting developments in shopping that people have noticed, experienced and talked about, and an unusual number of them have been led by Tesco. For a big business in an established industry we have been the first one prepared to make quite important changes in the way that we compete and go about our business. And because of the nature of the business, some of these are triggers for quite important social changes such as 24-hour shopping, the development of business on the internet, the creation of a Clubcard and supermarket banking.

Tesco has become one of the most benchmarked companies in the world. There are undoubtedly discrete areas where we do things differently from the rest of the world. It may be insight into customers or use of technology or retail branding or the development of fresh food and prepared goods or the development of the supply chain or people management. Whichever it is our methods are being scrutinised.

We take a lot of care in thinking about the way the business operates. Tesco has articulated very carefully its core purpose, which is to create benefits for customers so as to earn their lifetime loyalty. This means it should conduct all of its affairs so that a customer will notice things getting better in their life in some small way – more convenient shopping, safer food, or a more interesting shopping trip.

One of our key values is to understand the customer, so everything stems from an insight into customer's lives. This means you see change taking place in society much more quickly. Your response to that may look like an innovation, but actually it's a result of what you see happening.

The other key value is that we've got to innovate and be

the first to make customers' lives easier. We have made formal the fact that the business is prepared to operate to a higher level of risk than you might expect, because whenever you try and be first you're going to get a lot of things wrong. These values are not simply something you get out of a book and stick on a wall. They came out of the business looking at itself over literally hundreds of discussions involving thousands of staff. They wrote down the business that they recognised and, in part, the business they wanted it to be.

The staff have much higher expectations when you have strong corporate values because they expect the company to live the values. Every move you make, every word you utter, every policy you give out, is tested against those values. If you don't do it, the other 199,999 won't do it.

One of the things that's striking about Tesco's is the lack of paper. What we are good at is the management process of bringing people together. We're very good at managing in teams and getting people round the table who between them have exactly the right balance of skills to solve a problem. The organisation has enough experience and insight and knowledge to solve a problem or realise an opportunity, but that is seldom in one person or in one department. So we're good at sharing knowledge and managing skill sets. We also believe you should ask more than tell; an open listening style provides the basis for a tremendous amount of innovation. We have 200,000 people working with 12 million customers, and they know more about their lives and about the job than anybody else will ever know. So if you open up, they'll tell you what works well, what doesn't work well, and how it could be done better.

Praise more than criticise – it seems obvious but it's easy to forget how fantastically well people respond to praise. *'I appreciated that, you did a good job, do some more of it'* can make a huge difference in terms of how people feel about themselves and about coming to work. It makes them more prepared to take risks and more prepared to be engaged in what the business is trying to do. So the big prize is that you could potentially engage the combined creativity and talent of 200,000 people, rather than just the few.

We also say celebrate success but learn from experience. We actually said learn from failure, but our own staff didn't like the word failure and wanted experience instead. It is important because, if you really want to be first, a lot of what you try is going to be wrong and the thing that absolutely kills innovation is a bad reaction to somebody getting it wrong.

We use the word innovation because it suggests to people a process of applying creativity to change. It implies development and moving on, and it has a momentum and an edge. It's about growth. It is still creative because it is borne out of observation and a response to that, which is creative in the sense that it didn't exist before.

Being well managed, being spoken to, being motivated, being part of something that's winning and innovating, that customers like, and that is admired – all this has a powerful effect on the way people think. It also attracts people who want to work in a business that is accepting of change and risk taking. Others want to come and work here because we do internet business, or because of our database management, or because we're felt to be a leader in supply chain management. If you get a good reputation for leading edge thinking about a particular business practice, then you will attract people.

The nature of the business tends to determine the culture and the skills. People management is a very heavy responsibility at Tesco. The culture tends to be consensual, moving together towards a single vision. The organisation is serious and there is an intensity about it. We work out what we're trying to do as a business for the customer and then we create processes which involve and attach people to that. It's actually quite demanding in terms of conformity. It doesn't encourage mavericks but on the other hand if you're really listening to your organisation and you're really taking in all the ideas, a lot of those ideas are going to be uncomfortable. But being a marketing organisation where you take your cue from the customer can provide a tremendous rationale for change.

There does need to be structure but not a hierarchy in the old-fashioned sense of lines of command. Everybody needs to know exactly what job they're expected to do, how they're supposed to do it, that they're resourced to do it, trained to do it and that they'll be told how well they're doing in it. We give each of our 200,000 people two full reviews a year. For many of them it's the only time in their lives when they're told what they've done well or what they could do better. It is also a real meritocracy; we have people on the board who started as Saturday shelf stackers. There's no managerial elitism.

Overall I'm not sure creativity is sufficiently valued in this country. When I sit at the table with other Chief Executives or senior establishment figures, a lot of topics get discussed but rarely innovation. Many of the professions attract tremendously able people, but they don't put those people in situations where they have to create and innovate and take risks. To some extent the concept of a profession almost mitigates against creativity because it tries to set down, in any given situation, what is the right response. And many people from those professions have risen to high levels of management, whether it's accounting or the law.

I gave out the prizes at a very good girls' school recently and the brightest 25 out of 100 were all going to be doctors. Although I thought that was fantastic for the medical profession, a part of me felt that if the 25 of them went off into the wealth creating parts of life, then the medical profession might be better off ultimately because a stronger economy usually results in a better health service. There is still a tendency for the academic system to put its brightest people into areas other than business.

I have this impression that unlike America, most ordinary British people expect to earn a salary. They look for the place that will give them that salary for the longest period of time, like a good reputable company, a profession or the government. They still think in terms of *'I earn a wage and I live on a wage and I have some saving'*. Whereas I think the Americans have a more natural understanding of the concept of wealth creation, risk taking, profit investments and capital growth.

My advice to my children would be to take something which is very creative and intrinsically interesting for them, and see if there's a business application for it. For example, if you were interested in medicine there might be tremendous business applications, whether it's creating new medical equipment or creating a new medical service. Try to create something that is of greater value to society. That is often what a business application is. It takes something that's good and finds a way of making it more easily available.

I think as a nation we need a better understanding of the process by which wealth creation benefits society. There is too great a mental separation between good social works, a good quality of life and making money in this country. You make only as much money as is decent and then you go and do something worthwhile. Or you make a choice between making money and doing something worthwhile. They shouldn't be separated.

Take two family members, say a brother and a sister of equal ability, where one becomes a doctor and the other becomes a business person. Society sees the doctor as doing something that's more worthwhile. But it's important people understand that the progress of society, which gives them freedom, choice, well-being and all the things they want, can come out of economic progress. If we could change that mindset we would get a flood of talent into business and I think that would be terrific for the economy.

olish born American architect Daniel Libeskind stands at the forefront of a great resurgence in museum design. His buildings are instant architectural landmarks. Current projects include the daring £75 million spiral extension to the V&A and the Imperial War Museum of the North in Manchester. His first commission was the Jewish Museum in Berlin followed by another museum dedicated to the work of the Jewish painter Felix Nussbaum. In addition to his British projects he is working on a concert hall in Germany, another Jewish museum in San Fransisco and a university in Mexico, a corporate headquaters in Dresden and a convention centre in Tel Aviv.

Daniel Libeskind

There is a real collision taking place between art, culture, business and technology. The old tramline divisions no longer seem tenable. I think the public desire is not for artificial divisions but for a fuller participation in culture and its economy. The lines that used to divide activities mentally, physically and emotionally are being fused. There is an urge to see life as a modulated whole and not as a series of abstracted fragments which don't really fit together, or fit together in a very unrewarding manner. The need is for a more organic, seamless connection and greater continuity between traditions – future aspirations and past inheritance.

Where architecture is concerned, I don't buy into this notion of the architect sitting in his studio, doing designs and offering them up. For me, it's all about collaborating creatively with the public desire. It's never been a question of *'that's a nice design, go and build it'*. Architects compete with stone and concrete, but what is radical is what you can do with material reality to affect the mind and imagination of the participants. Each of my projects has been very sensitive, politically and historically, so it's a process of discourse and evolution. Engaging the public from the very beginning, however controversial it might be, is the real creative challenge.

Architecture is about business competition but it's also about winning the hearts and minds of people for projects that are innovative and that bring a completely new kind of economic possibility to an area. It integrates economics and culture. It also takes the power of the arts to give a compelling shape and drama to something new. I've been fortunate to work on projects which deal with regenerating urban areas; not just a building, but how a building completely transforms people's idea of its context, whether that's London, Manchester, San Fransisco or Berlin.

Even though we have only just moved from the 'modern' period of the 20th century to the 21st century, there is a changed perception of new technology, of work place, of responsibility, and of ethics. The world is opening up and architecture is wonderfully positioned to provide a new orientation, and to engage with the public on how to read reality.

I've just come from San Francisco where I presented my project for a new museum – part of an old power station which is one of the oldest buildings in San Francisco. In some ways it's like Tate Modern here, but I'm doing something radically different. It isn't a case of just restoring the bricks but of giving the public back a 19th century history that is not so obvious today; the history of power in relation to what power means now – electrical power versus new imaginative, creative power.

The main creative lesson I've learnt building museums is to never give up and to always believe in the public. Never be cynical, never believe that the public doesn't know, never speak down to people and think that they don't understand. They do understand very, very well and they do care; that's why they're so conservative and against the transformation of their environment. People may be radical on Wall Street, they may fly aeroplanes, they may listen to avant-garde music, but when it comes to their window, the horizon and the sky, they know that this is irreplaceable and fragile. I appreciate this, I feel fortunate in working with the public and I believe in the participatory democratic process.

We no longer live in a hierarchic society so I don't believe in the top down approach where you just get on with it or tell people what to do. I believe that people are extremely interested if you can open their eyes. This is essential in architecture because a building is not over when it's built; it's just beginning its life. It's not like a book that can be filed away, or a movie that you no longer see, or a sound you no longer hear. It's there, and unless it's good and communicates across time it's just a folly.

You have to be an optimist and a believer or you would be cynical and give up before you even started. I think the public have been underestimated in the last 300 years of 'modernity' because so much of it came from the idea of partitioning emotion and reason, and the specialisation of programmes. I think the holistic approach is far more humanistic and civilised. That's why people still go to see Shakespeare; the whole complexity is there and yet it remains human. Shakespeare and Montaigne offer a much better model than Descartes; those who would reduce architecture to schematic conceptual ideas are not fully connected to the fact that we have emotions and other desires.

I feel a tremendous responsibility to the people who will use these museums. I don't want them to feel, *'now I'm being educated, now I'm enjoying myself, now I'm going to look at something I wanted to see, now I'm seeing something unexpected'*. I want to create a seamlessness and a feeling that they are being appreciated, that this is for them. Also that they are not simply statistics on the charts of architects and planners but that they are true participants fundamental to the success of the project. You build that sort of trust through communication and by tuning into all the frequencies before you even start.

From very early on in the V&A project I evolved the vision with the planners, with English Heritage, with various critics and even with those who love Victorian architecture. And that actually fuelled the creative process. One knows intuitively and functionally what can be done, but others shape it, give it articulation and provide the differences within it that can open up the spaces. If it is a wilful exercise of some form it will just remain on paper and never get built. Radical projects need to be rooted; in fact the word radical actually means *of the roots*. If something has deep roots, then I think it can have a strong response and yet really move forward and change things. If it doesn't then it is simply outmoded and a slave to conventions.

You need a vision to have a creative collaborative process. If you don't, then you just have a bunch of specialists doing the work together and that's different because it's no more than the sum of operations. But a vision should never be a dictatorial or authoritarian idea which is imposed on others. A powerful vision should open new vistas and spark the creative impulses of others, providing a real impetus for people to get involved. Architecture is in the public realm, it requires large resources and huge teams so there is a real dynamic of involvement at work.

I didn't want to see the V&A as some sort of white elephant. I wanted to be in love with it. It was the Greeks who rightly said, *'it's all about wonder'*. The infusion of wonder is the beginning of the process. I needed to look up at the V&A in wonder, like at a tree or the sky, and love it. Where else in the world do you have a place that's been dedicated to the public good and to the idea that culture is the driving force of society? The Victorians never saw it as an institution for the passive resurrection of the past. They saw the past as inspiring a new level of creative competitiveness for the future. The spiral is very much aligned to those ideas; it doesn't mimic them and it's not nostalgic for that world, but it does take the boldness and courage and belief in the power of new ideas to move the world on. Archimedes said, *'give me a spot on which to stand and I will move the world'*. I believe that point is the culture of a place.

You can look at every site with wonder if you're interested in it. One simply has to be attuned. Even in San Francisco where you might think there was nothing there before, but there was because it used to belong to the Indians. That's the difference between architects who are simply interested in style or fashion and architecture that is formed organically and that unexpectedly develops its own direction.

Creative bravery always makes business sense. Opening up new horizons and new possibilities is always pragmatic. The imagination is dynamic and the economy is dynamic. The economy is possibly the most creative and mystical of all because it can't be shaped or moulded. It's constantly evolving and you have to be attuned to it. People at a high level of business decision-making have to be imaginative because, if they are not, they are already left behind. I agree with Walter Baring who said that besides the four elements of water, earth, air and fire, there is a fifth element and that is money. The five fundamental elements that are both mythological and the substance of the world.

For creativity to be elevated you have to want to create the best in the world, not the second or third best. And ambition needs to be matched with the hard work it takes to achieve that. I used to be a musical performer and I tell others that you can't just play music because you want to, you have to spend years and years practising on the keyboard. You have to know how to play the notes, otherwise you can never play the music; but you also have to play so well that you play the music and not just the notes. That analogy is true for all creative fields; that aspiration needs a purpose. It's not a senseless, competitive market, it's about goals and desire.

It is possible to do the impossible and succeed. If you have a possible dream, it's already somebody else's. The real creative effort is in doing things which have not been simulated elsewhere. It's not about marketing, it's about how to actually be at the cutting edge of the mind. People we now admire for this thought that they had failed. Read the letters of Michelangelo who thought he'd failed miserably. He hadn't, it was just he wanted something far greater. That's an incredible lesson in humility and real creative genius.

Ian Livingstone is Chairman of London-based Eidos Interactive, a fast growing developer/publisher of computer games with a turnover of more than £200 million and whose big success is Tomb Raider starring Lara Croft. Ian is a games addict and his real interest is in the content side – the characters and storylines that go into the games. Ian started Games Workshop in the mid 70s with his friend Steve Jackson. They then wrote the Fighting Fantasy series of interactive books in the 80s which have now sold over 14 million copies in 23 languages and in the 90s he moved into computer games. As Chairman, Ian oversees all of Eidos Interactive's creative work and games publishing output.

Ian Livingstone

My experience is that it's very easy to say no to new ideas. It's so easy in this business and other businesses to do the 'me too' products. Something comes out and the marketing people want yesterday's products rather than tomorrow's because they're a proven success. However, most copycats don't do as well as original titles. For example, as soon as Trivial Pursuit came out you got a million question and answer games mimicking it. But once the franchise is established that's usually the dominant one, the others fall away.

In the United States financial backers are much more ready to take a chance and less likely to be criticised for it. They accept that they might get some wrong and some right. If you say 'no' here, you've covered yourself, you haven't made any mistakes, you think you're being clever and you're not doing badly but you're probably not doing that well either. The creativity exists; finding the backers is the hard bit. You struggle more than in other countries. And the danger is creative people start going *'Oh, maybe I did get it wrong and maybe I'm no good any more and maybe I should stop being creative and do something else'* but you've just got to try and keep that self-belief going and over-ride the self-doubt.

The American economy's strong because they're willing to take chances and back ideas. They also have belief beyond themselves and put huge amounts of money into marketing. Here, on the other hand, we often see marketing as a waste of money. We have a lot of self-doubt as a nation – all a bit shy and reticent. We need to be less critical. We like people to do well but only so well, and then we don't want them to do that well any more, we want to see them take a bit of a knock.

In this country we need to show that we embrace the technology that supports gaming – teaching animation within the gaming environment and programming within the gaming environment. We've got film school, drama school etc. So why not computer games? We are the second largest entertainment industry in the world after all is said and done. It represents $20 million worth of sales of software alone. It's a very serious entertainment industry. It's second only to records. It's ahead of video. It's ahead of Hollywood.

In my experience creative people have to establish their own creative culture. Although this is quite a liberal looking corporate office, there is no development here, all development studios are off site. They are in small units and if they want to paint their walls black and hang plastic models of Marilyn Monroe and racing cars from the ceiling and put fluorescent paint all over their chairs, then that's fine because it makes them feel happy. There's no point trying to put creative people into a corporate environment and hoping they're going to be creative. It's important to keep them separate and let them do their own thing.

Having said that it's no longer two blokes in a garage. It can take six months before you can even vaguely figure out if the game's going to be any good or not, because you've got to build this very complex process. It's more like making a movie now because you've got 3-D programmers, 2-D programmers, artificial intelligence programmers, 3-D graphic artists, animators, speech, music, sound effects and video working together to create a seamless cinematic experience.

This obviously needs some structure and they have to work to a schedule and a budget. There's tight control there. But it needs to be run by producers who are very creative-friendly as you don't want to upset creative people. I think the more creative a person is, the more self-doubt they have and therefore the more vulnerable and sensitive. So you have to massage egos, make sure they're happy and cared for and given constant attention. If you give them a secure environment then you can maximise their creative potential. It's important to recognise that developing a computer game is a very frustrating, almost ethereal process.

Ruth McCall is a founder and former Managing Director of Cambridge Animation Systems, a company launched in 1990 to provide creative software applications for cartoon feature film and television production companies. The company is a leader in its field and won the Queen's Award for Exports in 1998. Previously, Ruth had worked for Carlton Communications plc, researching and producing television documentaries and later in management positions. She is interested in the application of humane and creative management practices within the commercial work environment. She has two children.

Ruth McCall

think creativity is in the pure arts; it's in writing, it's in painting, it's in musical and theatrical performance. I used to work in television and I don't regard that as a particularly creative industry, and I don't regard advertising as a particularly creative industry; I regard those as popular industries which have the tag 'creative' applied to them because it's useful for recruitment and it makes you feel good to be working with them.

Business creativity is applied and is determined by commerce. I see art and commerce as almost inimical to one another. Once you have creativity harnessed to commerce I don't see it as particularly creative any more. I know that there are people in the background with charts saying, *'ABCs only like blue curtains so for Heaven's sake get rid of the yellow ones'*. I didn't see television as creative, because it's all about ratings. In my world creativity is similarly determined by how many people want to do cartoons using software, and how many people want a button on the left of the screen rather than on the right.

I'm not sure how much modern creativity in the work place has to do with creating products. I find it interesting that software firms which regard themselves as doing a creative job, call themselves creative workers. Sometimes they say to me, *'I'm an artist and I can't be expected to be held to deadlines any more than any other artist and no, I don't know how long it will take'*. We had a very interesting argument with the software team about whether or not their work was in a sausage factory or painting the Sistine Chapel. This was actually an argument about whether they were part of a mechanical or industrial process over which they had no control and where no art was involved, or whether they were painting the Sistine Chapel where immense art and longevity was involved. As the managing director of the company – trying to impose deadlines, trying to get products out, trying to ensure that they work well and that they're packaged and that people want to buy them – I'm often accused of running a sausage factory. I tell them I'd like to see them painting the

Sistine Chapel, but there's got to be a bit of sausage factory to tell me whose going to be up the ladder when, and whether Health & Safety Regulations are being obeyed.

If you consider creativity to be a solitary artistic process, then I would argue that creativity only exists within pure arts. If creativity is a collaborative effort, then you could say that getting a software team to write a good product might be as challenging and as creative as getting the Corps de Ballet to perform their routine because it does involve a lot of communication and co-ordination so that the whole, when it emerges, is complete.

So for me business creativity is more to do with seeing how you can be creative for the people that you have working around you and how you can draw out their creativity. As we've stopped having industries based on might, and as every form of work depends more on communication and human relationships, you could say that creativity is sweeping across the whole working world. Business creativity is about how you work with people, how people work in groups, how people manage change, how people get satisfaction out of their working lives, and how well they are able to integrate their working lives into their whole lives. These are issues that are being tackled with a certain amount of innovation in the newer industries because they're not fighting rigid structures which have been there for a long time and it's creeping into those industries which are reinventing themselves all the time, so as not to be left behind.

I also think the involvement and development of women's roles in the work place is having an enormous impact on industry, because, although I think this could be challenged, I think we have chosen to work in slightly different ways from traditional male structures. I don't think women enjoy hierarchy so much and I don't think they need a pecking order that is defined in the old-fashioned manner as lines of command. I also think women work better in groups and are, perhaps, better able to do that because they've developed good communication skills.

Major status concerns and chain of command structures are deeply oppressive to creativity: being able to tell, for example, what everyone did by the kind of car they had in the car park, and how close that car parking space was to the main door, and how many windows their office had and whether they ate in the executive dining room, the staff cafeteria or the work tea room. That doesn't mean, however, that you can dispense with structure, I consider companies that don't have chairs on the grounds that the meetings last as long as people can stand up comfortably, equally odious.

There is almost a war of attrition going on between traditional structures and the new industries (especially dot.coms) where mass youth culture is taking over and it's not unusual to have a boss younger than some of the people they're managing. These people tend to be uncomfortable with a big car, a dual-aspect corner office and a seat at the board table. Instead they create environments where it can be difficult for others to know who's managing them. This is a problem we've had in our company, in that overdoses of democracy have led to everybody feeling that they're running the business.

The key to sustained commercial success is undoubtedly the quality of the relationship that a business manages to have with the outside world. Customers and how they feel about the product and what they want in it, and the sense of identification they have with the clan that uses that particular kind of product, are very important.

A lot of our customers like being Animo users and I believe we're very good at maintaining our relationships with the outside world. We hold training courses in the company for people who come to use this very complex design tool at professional level and that's a great bonding opportunity. The people that trained the trainees paid attention to getting to know them and getting to understand how they were using the software. They stayed friends and postcards were flying all around the world; people were moving from studio to studio and we tried to help them find jobs. There is a whole community of quite quirky people out there using our product. On those higher flights of fancy one could say that that way of working promotes world peace – it promotes people getting to know things they wouldn't have known and meeting people they wouldn't have met. I think that's a form of human creativity.

Our business evolved because there was a commercial interest in finding an area of the media world which hadn't been penetrated by technology. But I think with most products, as opposed to works of art, there are many links and collaborations with different bodies that lead to the creation of something new.

Software people however perceive the world as being like them. They'll say things like *'I deliberately didn't make it easy to change the shading – because I'm thinking, if it were me, I'd really very much prefer to write my own algorithms; so what I did was I just left it free, so that they could actually write their own algorithm and then perhaps create a little graph in which they would choose their own parameters…'* and I'm saying no, they just want to press light, dark or shaded, just like a photocopier. Software programmers don't realise that others don't want that degree of algorithmic control. So the creativity in working with software developers is in trying to get them to understand what it feels like to be a user who is very likely to have a completely different world view from them.

There is a lively battle that goes on between the banality of catering for the market and the desire of the software designers to leap far beyond that and to introduce to the market something that would challenge their mode of work. Sometimes it feels as if creative people dislike customers because they are so unwilling to try and tailor things to the needs of the outside world. I have to keep reminding people who work in software that we're a commercial organisation. Unfortunately we're not a university with an R&D wing devoted solely to challenging graphic problems, we actually have to get something finished and ready, that works, and has some boring bits attached to it which have to be done. There's a great desire in software always to work on what's cutting edge; people can get very fed up with working at the ordinary edge.

I don't think intense competitive pressure leads to more creative solutions, if anything I'd say it's the reverse. If there's a major swamping of stress because the company's not doing so well, they're not selling so much and the competitors seem to be doing better, people just tend to become gloomy. In my experience they don't rush off to their lab to try to find some wonderful solution.

Personal competitiveness: that works; somebody wanting to get something over somebody else who they think didn't really understand their way of doing it. That works enormously well and then people really go and show you what they're made of, and that has often been a really useful way of getting things dealt with effectively.

One of the problems with any company that starts from scratch and has to grow is that there's constant change going on and people really don't like change. The balance of people you need in a company and the kind of skills you need change all the time. The dot.com industries are not that different from software companies, we're all living from hand to mouth and writing a five year business plan is simply writing in the sand. The trick is to make sure it looks credible enough to get investors to think it would work.

Small companies are intrinsically more creative and flexible. Getting your message from the message creator to all the message receivers is immensely more straightforward. My company is about 30 people, it's been at about 70. We've now started working much more actively with other partners to replicate some of the roles that we formerly did within our own group. Business allegiances and alliances with other organisations is part of what enables small companies to move on. I think small companies in modern industries learn to change all the time as part of their process of survival, because you're much closer to things not working out, and so therefore you pause all the time to think, why are we doing that? what are those five people working on? is there any benefit in it? perhaps we should stop that and move on to something else?

I think there is a particularly British brand of business creativity and it's to do with the fact that we had this empire a hundred years ago and we dominated the world. There's a certain cultural propensity on the part of the British to work creatively with people of all kinds. We have quite a multi-cultural society and we are used to people from all sorts of places coming to live here by right. Even as colonials I think the British may have had a degree more patience with the local cultures than some of the other colonial powers and we may have retained some links that have proved useful over many years. I do think working successfully with the rest of the world is about understanding other cultures, being tolerant of the way other people work and being seen to be fair and reasonable. Some of the British characteristics which may seem old fashioned now, are about being fair. I don't think British industry is particularly corrupt; I have never been offered any kind of bribe. I've been offered a nice lunch now and again, but I've never been offered anything that could be remotely construed as a bribe. Nor have we ever in our dealings with anybody offered bribes. I do think that there is a reputation that still attaches to British industry in the world. People find us relatively easy to deal with. It's those basic qualities: fair play, decency, honesty, being nice to people, trying a lot harder to help people out, being reliable, they count for an enormous amount in this shaky world. And they count even more in the creative world because it's such a fragile, scary world of deadlines and sudden crises erupting, and you're terribly dependent on the goodwill of your suppliers and partners.

Since the war it's been considered very sexy to work within the creative industries. There's prestige attached to people who work in advertising, television or graphic design; very little attaches to people who work in marketing or sales. In this country it's still difficult to find people who respect the creativity of the sales process. In America they love selling, they don't despise it; they make it a creative process and admire people who thrive doing it well. I have many people come to my company who I think could be great salesmen because they have a very engaging personality, they're very quick and they're smart, but they just say, *'Work in Sales? God no'* because they can't imagine telling their friends that they work in sales. That would be a humiliating step down from everything they aspire to. When people start saying to me: *'I want to work in sales, I'm brilliant at it, I do deals here there and everywhere, I could bring a lot to your company…'* then I will start to believe that things are changing. I'm still not having anybody say that.

I would also say that the Americans are much better at management. They experiment with different forms. In contrast we create these strange embarrassment-driven, lack-of-structure organisations because we can't cope with a situation of *'I'm the boss, we do it like this, you come in at seven and I expect you to leave at four, in between those times I want to see this, this , this and this finished'*. That's why I'm quite intrigued to see what happens to some of these dot.com companies as their structures grow, and they accumulate, as every company does, people who don't work very effectively.

Business has been seen as second-best in this country for a long time. I think it's only in the last 20 or 30 years that business people have become popular, glamorous individuals. I

think Richard Branson has done a wonderful thing by glamor-
ising endeavour. But people who have done well with money
are tremendously envied and the British way of envy is to
decry, revile, humiliate and pretend they don't want it. There is
still a huge amount of envy sweeping around in British society.

If you accept that capitalism is the prevailing economic
structure that we live with and that we're going to be working
within, then you have to accept that capitalism is fuelled by
wanting to be the winner in the marketplace. There is creativity
in selling and in managing and these are some of the new cre-
ativities which I think go towards making a successful, winning
organisation.

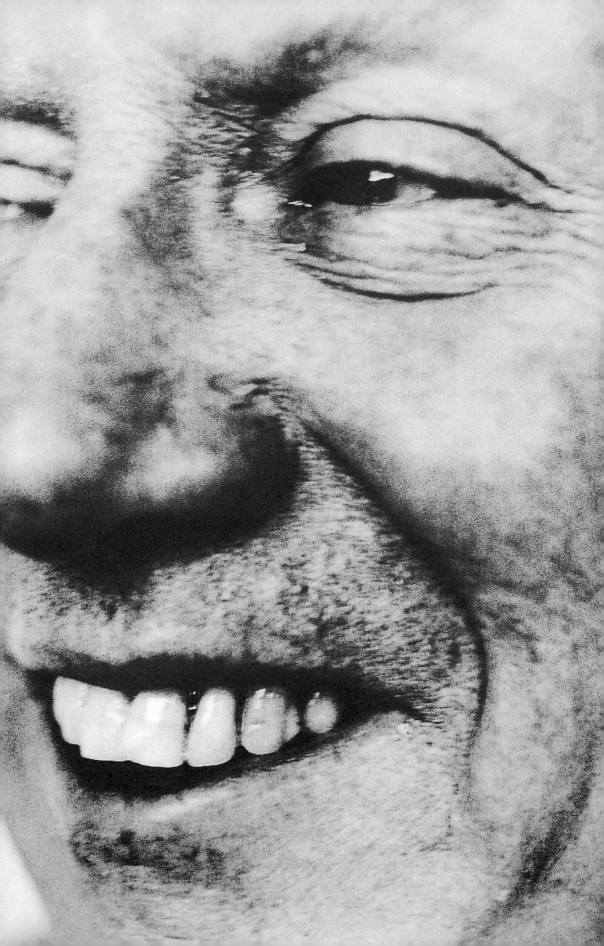

Michael Perry

Michael Perry is currently Chairman of Centrica plc. Centrica was formed in February 1997 following the demerger of British Gas plc. It trades as British Gas within England and Wales and Scottish Gas in Scotland, the Automobile Association and Goldfish. The group employs around 30,000 people.

Michael Perry is also Chairman of Dunlop Slazenger Group Ltd and Deputy Chairman of Bass plc. In 1996 he retired as Chairman of Unilever plc after 39 years of Unilever service which included serving as Chairman of Unilever subsidiaries in Thailand, Argentina and Japan.

In 1994 he received a knighthood in recognition of his services to industry and export.

After the war the world economy went through a period of massive change and the Japanese were amongst the first to realise that business was going to be about what I call *the creation of market preference*. Right from the word go businesses were going to have to understand what it was that would *create* preference. And where you see that most is in the new start-up company. If it has got off the ground then it has already demonstrated its relevance by having created a position of preference.

Competition forces one to re-fight the battle of winning preference constantly. The companies that fail or flounder are often those which have rested too long on their past laurels and have forgotten that they have to fight the battle for preference every shopping day.

Unless the customer benefit theme is going right through the whole creative process, you will not end up by producing creative innovation that is relevant. In the early years of computers, the computer people produced the most fantastic gizmos and we all cast about desperately trying to think of what to do with them. Nobody had thought that through properly. In those days computer design businesses were immensely creative, but in ways which were not really focussed on end users. Then along came the likes of Mr Gates and suddenly it was transformed. An early breakthrough in this was Akio Morita of Sony who was a great electronics engineer. It suddenly occurred to him and his team to focus on what customers might want out of all his kit – and they realised it was something they could put in their pocket. The Sony Walkman was an extraordinary breakthrough in applied technology at the time, and it was creative because it applied known technology to a specific identification of customer needs, and so revolutionised everything that was taking place in that field. Bill Gates did the same for software. Before him nobody built software with the same intensity of understanding for customer needs satisfaction.

Creativity is on two planes. There's the pure creativity with which people find new ways of designing products, components, systems or processes and then there's the creativity which finds a way of applying those innovations competitively. The British problem is that we have always scored better in the first area. We've been amongst the greatest creators and inventors in the world but we've been a lot less successful in fitting our inventions precisely to users' needs.

I had direct experience of this when I was with the British Overseas Trade Board, trying to hawk British products around the world. I remember when NEC in Japan were in the market for two major pieces of equipment and they bought one from us and one from the Germans. They told us ours was better built and better designed but that the German equipment actually did what they wanted it to do. The Germans had made a greater effort to understand NEC's needs and adapt their equipment to it, whereas we said we had the best piece of kit available and implied that if there was a problem, it was NEC's problem not ours.

That was symptomatic of an attitude which was very pervasive in this country. It probably stemmed from a hugely successful colonial past when we did make the best things and we shipped them to all those grateful people out there, and they were only too delighted to pay us handsomely for the privilege of being allowed to use an English made product.

I was responsible for a piece of research in Japan amongst Japanese industrial buyers which sought to compare their views on various aspects of company performance between companies originating from various OECD countries. In other words, what they thought about a product which came from Germany or France or the UK or the United States. We came out surprisingly high in their judgement on quality – that was not a problem – and also, to my amazement, on after sales service. But we were the bottom of the heap on marketing. We were considered to be the worst of the lot, and by marketing they meant products designed to meet their specific requirements.

I think the day of the customer has now finally arrived in this country. We now have a thoroughly competitive gas industry, for example. There are something like 25 suppliers from whom you can choose, but of course what comes hissing down the pipe is the same for everybody, and it comes down the same pipe and it probably comes from a similar source. So what matters in generating preference are all the things to do with associated services and customer attention.

Youth is, I believe, of huge significance in the whole process of creativity. I always thought that the most important thing that one could do was to empower the young people in your business to do creative things. What matters is how close the business is to young people in their social environment, in the coffee shops or the bars. Understanding not only where they are now, but where they're going to be in 5 or 10 years time because your development cycle always takes three or four years in the making. If the most serious buyers of cosmetics are women between the ages of 17 and 23, and if you want to be in the forefront of research and development, with its four-year cycle, then the people whose minds you've got to understand are 13 today. You need to know how to be ready with what they want in four years' time. Other young people will inevitably be closer to their thinking.

One of the most successful shampoos ever designed was Timotei. It came out of the heart of Scandinavian culture where the brand team was into themes like flower power, innocence and peace. It was a theme which over the following few years struck a chord right across the world.

By and large the willingness to change diminishes with age and people are at their most flexible and impressionable when they're young. So you can nearly always sell a new idea more easily to a young person than to an older person.

Young people can also be more willing to take risks on their own account. Maverick entrepreneurs are often young, like the people who, before the dot.coms, started firms like Stagecoach or

The Body Shop. People who join companies like mine and the companies I've always worked for, are people who would be less willing to take risks on their own account. Almost by definition, you're more willing to take risks on your own account when you have less at stake, like families, houses and mortgages.

Successful risk takers are those who have, through creative processes of some kind, achieved a preference strike. The Body Shop created preference in its time by selling the same sort of things as Boots, but calling them natural and ethical. Through brilliant sparks of marketing ingenuity it created something that felt very different and in tune with the times. Creative geniuses, like Anita Roddick and Richard Branson, need to be risk takers and are likely to act on their instincts when they are young.

Effective marketing can create enormous excitement and expectation but you will not be creating preference unless you can deliver and live up to the promise. If there's no sustainability about the competitive advantage, it can't survive much beyond the prime first mover advantage. I suspect the big winners on the internet are going to be established businesses who grab the opportunity to put in place internet adjusted systems of electronic communication which will help the process of delivering existing preference.

In a big corporation it's difficult to replicate the buzz which comes from building your own thing and taking your own risks. But the move away from the concept of lifetime employment and fixed salary into variable pay with very high rewards for great success on an individual basis is a step in that direction. I think it's true to say that the balance of ambition has shifted dramatically in my business lifetime. When I came into business 50 years ago the main thought was to have a career where you could go through until the end of your days and then pick up a nice pension. You put your career in the hands of the company who employed you, and then, if you were very good, you got promoted; if you weren't you didn't and on the whole you accepted it. Nowadays people's expectation of alternative developments for their career is much greater and they take their own career development much more in hand.

Five or ten years ago many companies drew the wrong conclusions from this. They drew the conclusion that they shouldn't expect to retain people, that if people were not being fulfilled they'd move on. That was when things like portable pensions were invented. But companies suddenly found they had no continuity of management. The cumulative experience of the company was being lost. Lessons were having to be learnt all over again every two or three years by another clutch of people coming to the business and things like loyalty, which go with continuity, were suffering. Of course no one should be working for anybody else if they don't think that mutual interest is being served. But when you've got a situation where people by and large don't put their first priority into doing what's right for the business they're in, but in doing what's right for them, then you have a problem. So the issue became one of rebuilding continuity and loyalty, but not at the expense of flexibility. New types of informal contract needed to be established between people – what is it we expect of each other and how can we make that mutually beneficial? It seems to me that all those areas are being creatively re-examined.

The culture of Unilever is very decentralised. You don't succeed in fast moving consumer goods unless you have massive creativity and flexibility. Empowering the local operator on the ground is critical. There have been times when clever thinkers thought that with the advent of globalisation, centralisation would make everybody much more efficient. But that overlooks the fact that people in Milan tend not to think, eat or behave in quite the same way as people in Oldham, and if you don't celebrate those differences in what you do, then you won't retain preference. Keeping people in power who are close to customers is the culture of the business. The Unilever philosophy is always to say to the local person *'you're in charge of the operating business, we'll set your objectives, but how you achieve them is up to you'*.

A good example of allocating responsibility at operational level is the story of CK1. Years ago we bought a firm called Calvin Klein Cosmetics, which produced fine fragrances under licence from Calvin Klein. It turned out to be the most successful fragrance business the world has ever seen. It was, and by and large still is, run by the same team of women. There were very few implants from Unilever because these very creative people only had one thing missing, and that was the financial clout to implement their ideas. At a certain moment they recognised that there was a creative opportunity in the area of fragrances for use by both men and women. Young people were dressing the same way, cutting their hair in the same way and because they understood the culture, they saw that gender stereotypes were changing. But fragrances are sold in department stores like Saks and Macys and young people don't go to those sorts of places. So where did they go? They went to record shops, to places like Tower Records, and in recognising this, Calvin Klein Cosmetics totally revolutionised the distribution system for young people's fragrances. CK1 became the most sold fragrance of our time. That for me was real creative thinking.

I feel there is no more creative, stimulating and exciting function than marketing because in a sophisticated company that is where ideas are started and the seed corn established. Then the whole thing is developed, through all the other functions of the business, to the final cut. Being the custodian of the customer's interest is what marketing is about. It requires massive attention to detail and it requires enormous creativity and inventiveness because every time you get on top of the heap, there will be a dozen others trying to push you off it, and at least four of them will succeed unless you keep on moving the heap. That's the name of the marketing game. I can't think of anything more exciting than when you achieve that.

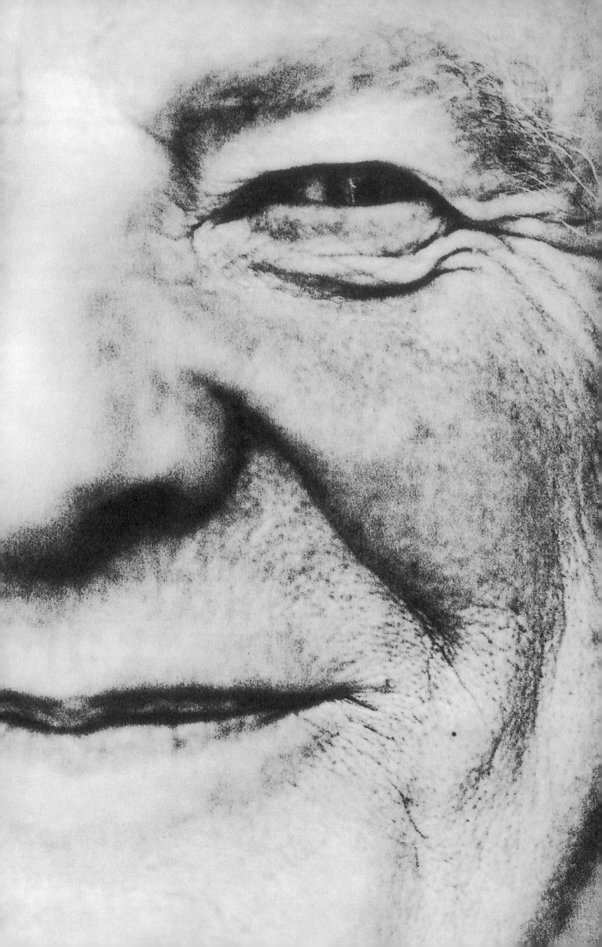

Brian Pitman joined Lloyds bank in 1952. In 1983 he became Chief Executive, and then Group Chief Executive of the new Lloyds TSB Group in 1995. In 1997 he was appointed Chairman. Lloyds TSB employs 80,000 people and in 1999 reported a profit before tax of more than £3.6 billion.

Brian Pitman was voted Financial World European Banking CEO in 1993; 1996 Times Businessman of the Year; 1998 KPMG Business Leader of the Year and was the winner of the 1999 Gold Medal of the Institute of Management.

He is Chairman of Next, a Director of Carlton Communications and a past President of the British Bankers Association and The Chartered Institute of Bankers. In 1994 he was knighted for his services to banking.

Brian
Pitman

We talk about living in a time of change but change implies a process of evolution. What we're experiencing is much more than that; we are faced with abandoning many of the things we have done in the past. Abandonment is a much more difficult task to accept than simply change. What we are managing today is not evolution or rapid change, we are managing transformation.

This puts an enormous premium on creative ideas because business success is determined by anticipating the future. Every business has to have ideas – it should have far more than it has the resources to cope with – and it should have the courage to implement them. We've got 80,000 employees all with their own ideas about how the business should be run. Young people in the organisation, in particular, want to change the world and you'd be mad not to listen to them because they've frequently got the best ideas for the future. They're not cluttered by the past, as so many of us are.

People will always have creative ideas, but in a big organisation you have to find a way to unleash that energy. What is needed is a discipline that's not heavy handed, that can encourage those ideas to come to the surface. Because, let's face it, people don't get up in the morning thinking, *'today what I'll do is put up a good idea to the Chief Executive and see how it works'*. Life's not like that.

So our means of tapping this ranges from incentivised suggestion schemes through to a strategy development scheme for section heads. The latter scheme involves section heads coming up with three different strategies in answer to the question, *'What exactly do we do that's different from the competition and how will this enable us to create value?'* And they have to put a value on each one. Our belief is that there's always a better strategy, it's just that you haven't thought of it yet.

I think if we said to people we want you to be creative, they may think that's not for me, that's for people who have a ponytail and behave completely differently from me. Whereas if we say we want you to come up with a strategy, or with ideas that are different from the competition, then they understand that very clearly. It's often those small things that really matter to the customer and can make a big difference to the business. It's something which customers value highly and are willing to pay more for because they're getting what they want.

There are many ways in which you can make a difference; it's not necessarily something which requires a huge break-through. In Hong Kong it was selling houses using virtual reality so that buyers could inspect the bathroom and experience the view of the Thames from the window without leaving Hong Kong. We were the first to offer this and it made a difference. With travel insurance it was recognising the anxiety people over 70 feel when insurance companies won't cover them for going overseas and extending cover to meet their needs. With children's clothes it may be that it has three rows of stitching rather than two, and so feels that much better. It may sound like very modest creativity, compared with some of the blinding creativity of, say, developing a car, but it's these little things that really make the difference for people.

You need to encourage people. So you have to make sure that whatever idea is put forward, you give it a response. That's absolutely vital. If people put a suggestion forward and they don't get a response – even if it's negative and you explain why you're not going to do what is suggested – they'll think it's a waste of time. And you've got to celebrate the good ideas, reward them and make sure everyone knows. We have an award system which we publish and in some cases we have an award ceremony. It's not really about the money, it's about people wanting to be recognised and feel that they really did do something that counted. They want a pat on the back.

The staff understand the customers better than anybody else. They are the best market research one can buy; they know whether things are going well or not. They know whether the customer is happy with us or not and if you don't take great notice of what frontline staff are saying to you the whole time, then you won't be successful.

They know, for example, that when you're granting a mortgage to people, often the biggest help you can give is to pay the legal fees. In many cases, it's more important than some fraction off the interest rate. If you haven't got any money and you're buying your first flat the real barrier is finding £2,000 for legal fees. People's needs are often not what you'd expect.

If you don't have a culture of innovation you might as well not be around as a business. The world moves on, people deliver things in different ways and so you can't stand still. You have to encourage people in a company like this, which is a very old established company, to behave in a different way. You try to preserve the things that were good, but you need to evolve because the world just keeps moving on. The status quo is the big problem. There's no doubt that when you start changing things, the good old days look better and better. And the more rapid that change, the more effort goes into preserving the status quo. You have to be prepared for massive resisitance.

You can't change a company by simply issuing instructions or by mission statements on video. In my experience, you can only change behaviour by changing beliefs. If people believe one thing, they'll behave in accordance with those beliefs. If people think we're in for a fairly easy time over the next five years, they'll behave in one way. If they believe we're fighting for survival in the next five years or might not be around in five years from now, they'll behave in a different way. So the task for the people at the top of any organisation in leadership terms is to level with people; to be completely honest and frank with them. I can't overemphasise the importance of being open – people can take the bad news, but they can't deal with deception.

There's nothing like a crisis to change an organisation. But management ought not to be managing for a crisis to create action. You need to involve people, to get them to participate in the issue so they really understand why it is that they cannot go on as they have in the past. It's about engaging in discussion with people back and forth across the organisation.

If I'm going to Liverpool, I will arrange to meet 20 staff in that area, and we chat in a room. It's an absolute free for all. They tell me what's wrong with the company, what we ought to do here, what we ought to do there. You get it straight from the shoulder. If you speak to a manager, he's proud and he won't want you to think there's even the slightest error in the business. The people who really tell you the truth are the staff. So you've got to have genuinely open communication both ways. If you live in a secret organisation, then you won't bring about change. Politics in a big organisation like ours is death. We desperately try to avoid internal politics; it's extremely bad for business.

One of the ways we use to stay ahead is to set ourselves exceptionally ambitious goals – what some people would call unreasonable goals. In the 80s we set ourselves the target of doubling the shareholder value of the company every three years. It was an idea that we got from Coca-Cola. We've now done it for 16 years despite the fact that it's a very difficult thing to achieve. When we started on this road we were worth £1.2 billion and we're now worth £36 billion.

Setting these ambitious goals forces the organisation to dig deeper for creative solutions and to rethink how the business should be run. It doesn't permit incremental thinking; the objective is to win, not just to improve. The challenge itself brings forth new ideas and new excitement. It encourages out-of-the-box thinking. As a result of the new energy and ideas stimulated by the challenge, the gap between the required and current performance somehow gets filled.

It's equally true at a personal level. I'm a keen golfer and if I said I was happy with a 24 handicap but I'd quite like to get it down to 18, that wouldn't be a very ambitious approach. If I set myself a goal of a handicap of 10 instead of 24, that would be more difficult to do. I might not get to the 10, but I might get to 12. That would be a lot better than 18. If you set these goals and, as a result, the staff achieve more than they ever thought they could achieve, they will feel good about themselves. That sense of achievement, whether it's climbing Everest or learning how to operate a PC when you're 60 and thinking you can't do it, is one of the most stimulating things for people.

We have a university here – the Lloyds TSB University. It's related to the business but it's for anyone and it's all about self-improvement. If you can improve people's self-esteem and sense of fulfilment, then you can really affect their behaviour. People will be more imaginative and creative if they feel good about themselves. So you need to create an environment for people where they can be achievers and setting ambitious goals is part of the process of getting there.

Staff are also highly motivated by customer satisfaction. If I get a letter praising Mabel in the Newport branch, I'll write back to the customer and I'll write to Mabel. The fact that the customer has gone to the length of writing to me at Head Office to say how wonderful she is will undoubtedly put a spring in her step.

We also believe in enabling people to work differently and I think we are a leader in this. We've got what we call Work Options which aims to make flexible working a reality for our staff. It positions flexible working as a mainstream business practice – not an entitlement or benefit – which involved seriously re-thinking the way we do business. And it has been amazingly successful – not just with women but with men too, and not just at the lower grades either. The way it works is that as far as we possibly can, we let people work whatever hours they want to work and we try to accommodate them in whatever places they want to work.

We've satisfied a lot of people's aspirations to balance their home and work lives which has meant that we've retained people who might otherwise have left and increased the commitment of others. So for example, some people want to work from 4 o'clock in the afternoon until 10 o'clock at night – it might sound unusual in a bank – but those are their personal circumstances. If you can arrange that for them, they are very, very grateful to you. It's fantastic for making people more effective and giving them more options in their lives and more control over it. There's a whole host of reasons why people might want flexible work options. And if they get it, they're usually determined to show that it will work.

Having said that we don't want people whose only contact with others is via a modem, so we do organise to bring people together so that they can stimulate one another with different ideas and know that they're appreciated.

We try hard in this company to create an environment where people can grow, and within a framework of creating value for shareholders, allow them the freedom to do their own thing. The world has moved on from the command/control structure and paternalistic style. Obviously we need some framework within which they can operate or everybody would be dashing off in every direction under the sun, but if you don't create an environment where people can experiment and have ideas – some which will work and some which won't – you won't make progress. And we try our utmost to avoid what we call a 'blame culture' because when you're experimenting, you make mistakes. What you've got to do when you've made a mistake is admit it, pick up the bits and pieces, write it off and get on with the next thing. We make many mistakes and I would be sorry if we didn't because then we wouldn't be sufficiently ambitious. We wouldn't be willing to explore opportunities.

If you're ambitious and you want to be the best in the world it puts you in a different league. It places you in a very stimulating environment. You meet other people who are equally successful on the world stage and that's very exciting because there's a cross-fertilisation of creative ideas and you constantly pick things up from others.

As a nation we're much more meritocratic now but we need to develop a culture of winning. There is often still envy rather than support for success here. We have tremendously successful people in this country, particularly and in individual activities such as the arts and sport. But when it comes to business, few shoot for the moon. A lot of people here are very satisfied with a modest level of achievement; the drive isn't always there to go on and do better and greater things. Yet we need highly successful business people to create the wealth for the country to prosper.

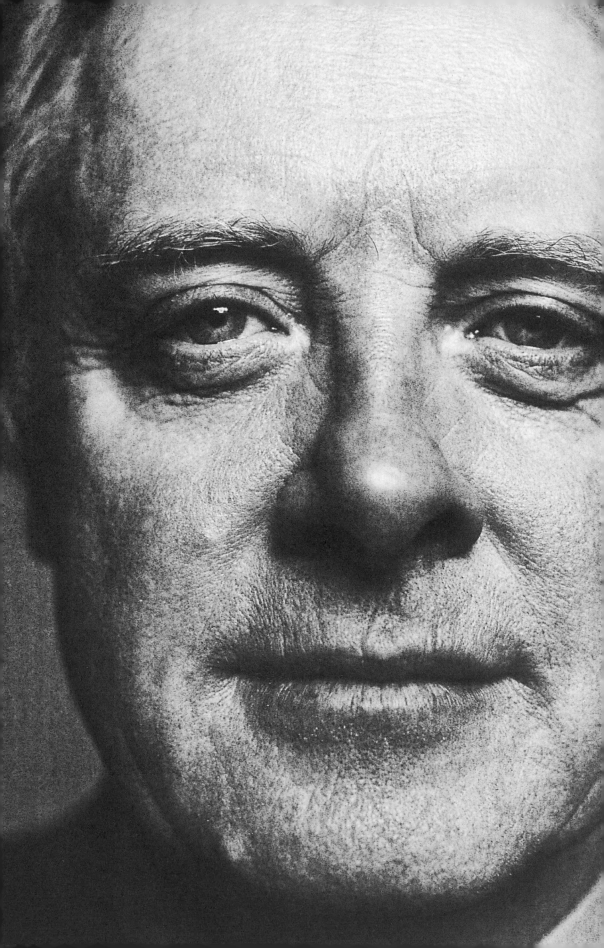

Gerry Robinson joined Granada in October 1991 as Chief Executive and took over as Chairman in 1996. The Granada Group spans broadcasting, programming, pay TV, technology, restaurants and hotels, and has a turnover of more than £4,000 million. He is also Chairman of the Arts Council and has been Chairman of BSkyB and ITN. Prior to Granada, Gerry was at Grand Metropolitan where in 1987 he led the UK's then largest management buy-out with the £163 million purchase of the Contract Services division which was later floated on the market as The Compass Group.

Gerry Robinson

'm a great believer in just sitting and chatting about a problem and involving other people. It's extraordinary how a thing can twist in the telling and you can come out with a solution which you might never have thought of in the normal run of things and which very often completely solves the problem. Creative solutions often come out of processes that really weren't intended to create that output in the first place. The same can happen if you leave a problem alone and come back to it later. So, by definition, I don't think creativity can be prescribed. There's no mechanism for getting at creativity.

There are people who are very creative and they can be quite disruptive since they are not followers of neat packages and they often don't fit very well into organisations that have a regimental approach to how things happen. A prescriptive approach to how things are done will inevitably restrict their creativity.

When some fundamental change happens in an industry, it gets creative. The whole telecommunications/telephone/television business is a good example, where the scene has changed dramatically in three years – the method of getting to the audience has changed, the number of channels has changed, the way that people view has changed, the connection between the net and telephony and computers, all of that has changed. But in a more commonplace way, it also happens when you take people out of the businesses that they're used to and put them into something new. I am a huge believer in taking talented people out of something where they've already proved themselves and getting them to run something completely different. Like moving Charles Allen from being in charge of the leisure division to running the TV side of the business because he's a very inventive man. Often you change roles for someone, and you find it's the thing that they desperately wanted to happen. You hit exactly the same issues in different businesses where people say *'you know I'm sorry you can't do this here'* and actually you've heard it 20 times before and the truth is you can.

It's not invention in the sense of something coming from nowhere, but taking lessons from one area and applying them in a different situation and having an inkling that it can work here too. Look at the work of Monet, he didn't do one haystack, he did 57 haystacks and actually he followed the work of someone else who did something very similar. Bill Gates is a business version of the same thing – his passion for computers and what they can do and why; he stayed at it, slogged away at it and had like-minded people working on it; all the things that made him a success. Doggedness is much underestimated.

Creativity has a lot to do with hard slog. People will find ways if *'I can't do it'* or *'it can't be done'* is not an acceptable answer. A doggedness about finding a way round often results in very creative output.

Running an organisation is really about having a few things you know you want to achieve and constantly coming back to those things that matter and knowing that if you don't achieve them, you've failed. Taking over LWT is an example, when everyone thought we would go for Yorkshire; but if what you really want to do is influence what happens in ITV, then you have to be prepared to take the risk of doing it. You need to be dogged and be able to deliver. Once you're clear in your own mind about what you're going to do and once you have a reputation for delivering based on actual delivery, then you're pretty much there. Confidence breeds confidence and it's amazing how quickly it can turn things round. Single leadership is key and I don't just mean that as the head of the company. If the person who runs programme making at Granada Television is absolutely passionate about putting more programmes on the air because they make the best possible programmes, it will make a big difference.

It's so important not to try to over-manage an organisation. People think it's about control, but its not. You don't prescribe how to make things happen, you enable them to happen. I often find that people achieve something in ways that I would not have given a hope in hell's chance of working. You know, they've just done it in a completely different way and you're astounded that somehow they've made it work. It's not how I would have done it but they've made it happen and that's fine as far as I'm concerned. You must allow people to do things in their own way and judge it by the output. That's far more important than whether someone's like you, or whether you like that individual.

Take a company like Granada. You are looking at a very small central team, where there are 32 of us, including secretaries and drivers. We can't sit here and tell the rest how best to make television programmes or what's the best possible way of running Little Chef. You need to create a genuine feeling in the organisation so people feel *'I know what I'm doing here, leave me alone and it'll be all right, I'll make it work'*. You stand a much greater chance of keeping talented, creative people if you leave them alone. And I think that's true across all industries, because a lot of the fundamentals are about getting people fired up, getting them feeling, more than anything else, that if they make it work it gets noticed.

They are the ones doing it, it's not some prescribed central plot that they simply have to colour in. In businesses that aren't well run you often hear things like, *'well it fell on a Sunday'* or *'the weather was lousy'*. A sense that there's nothing you can do about it. People come to work because they want it to be exciting, they want their lives to be interesting and they want to be noticed and make an impact. So I don't think what I'm talking about is fighting against the grain.

With the Arts Council I was dealing with a very government, civil servant-like set of circumstances where it can be difficult to make decisions quickly or to get people to change. In addition it was a dispirited organisation that hadn't had any additional money for 10 years, which makes it difficult to be creative. Talented people who have a lot going for them by and large don't stay in an organisation that doesn't allow them to express themselves.

At first the Arts Council didn't have the mechanics in place which help you to know what's happening, what's going on and what the issues are. That doesn't rest with just one person, it must rest within the organisation, so that at the appropriate level, whoever's in charge, actually knows what is working well and what isn't. The Arts Council now employs fewer people, is far more effective and has a passion about it and a real sense that you can make a difference. Now when we say *'if only we could find another £10,000 for the LSO we could have this fantastic tour of the West Country'* there's belief that we're going to make it happen because it really is important.

Part of getting more money is about having a vital, confident organisation that is prepared to speak up and say *'No – sorry that's not valid from our point of view unless A, B, C, D, E happens'*. Its amazing how much more comfortable people feel with that approach despite the fact that we all shilly-shally around saying *'well you'd better not say that to Charlie'*. What you should say to Charlie is: *'look I'm sorry Charlie but you know this isn't working and unless it changes we're all going to have a problem'*. And Charlie's actually a much happier man.

Of course you can get it wrong and we get it wrong all the time, but provided you're willing to change and alter I think that can work for you. I recently had lunch with somebody who talked to me about all the things I'd been involved with that hadn't worked. I didn't remember any of them. We have this fantastic capacity after the event to make it better than it was. But if you want people to have a crack at things, they must be able to make mistakes and not be penalised for it. Covering up a mistake tends to compound the problem whereas correcting it could result in an imaginative solution you simply didn't expect.

I think if you're interested in business, it's important to see the whole picture early on. If the business is turning over £1 million the principles and issues are fundamentally the same as if it's turning over £1 billion. Seeing how the whole thing hangs together, how sales works alongside product design and how marketing works alongside how you're going to finance your production process. You're more likely to see the whole picture early on if you work within a small outfit. There is a case for large organisations being made up of lots of small organisations. If you look at our education business, a tiny little business that we acquired with Yorkshire, it was allowed to grow and develop itself with a couple of dozen people. It now employs a couple of hundred and it would not have felt the heavy hand of Granada at all. So that's an example of something within a large business which is really a small business. But I think that is still relatively rare.

I think Britain has been astonishingly successful in the international business game. British businesses have a very good capacity to be creative. Creativity has rarely been the problem. The problem has often been the follow-through.

There is still a sense that business is not a good use of your time and that academia is more important. High quality people still end up in the civil service, wasting themselves, whereas given a proper opportunity in a business environment they could achieve a great deal.

But I'm no great fan of the American model. America seems so effective, it is a large market and a lot of it does work but it doesn't have the same creative capacity to correct when it goes wrong. It's brilliant when everything works but they're very resistant to doing things differently or coming at an issue from a different angle. I spent a lot of time looking at Coke operations around the States. What I found was that they were not inventive problem solvers. It was a case of *'this is how you do it, that's how it works, so off you go'*. The guys delivered it to the supermarkets proudly and fought PepsiCola for space, polished the bottles and put on the price bursts. But hit a problem and they really floundered.

In the States they hugely revere business success which they relate to how much money you make. But how can that be so central? It's far more important that you make a good job of how you bring up your children, or the relationships you have with your friends or your family. It's much more balanced and rounded here. Yes, business is important, and it's very important that we do it well and that we're inventive and sharp and able, but at the end of the day it's only business, not the be all and end all.

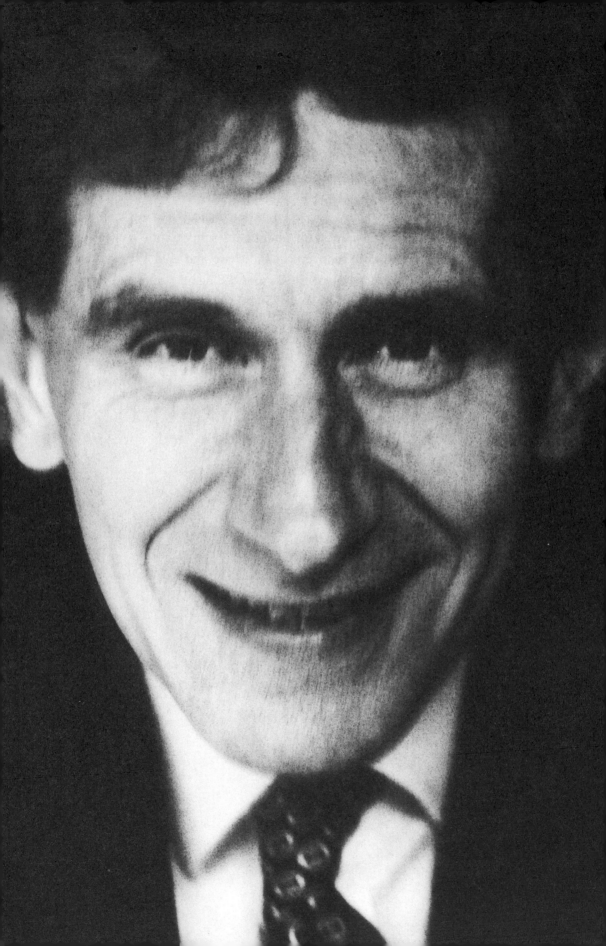

Dennis Stevenson is Chairman of Pearson plc, AerFi Group (formerly GPA Group) and Halifax plc. From 1988–1998 he was Chairman of the Trustees of the Tate Gallery. He is now Chairman of the Tate Gallery Foundation and he sits on the board of the British Council. He is one of two outside members of the Takeover Panel appointed by the Governor of the Bank of England to represent industry. He headed the Stevenson Commission set up by Tony Blair to examine the role of information technology in schools and was subsequently appointed to be the Prime Minister's advisor on the application of IT to education. He was made a CBE in 1981 and became Lord Stevenson of Coddenham in 1999. He sits on the cross-benches in the House of Lords and has recently been appointed Chairman of the new House of Lords Appointment Commission.

Dennis Stevenson

grew up in a world in which people involved in the creative arts were only concerned with creative excellence. They wanted to produce the perfect opera or exhibition first and then work out how to pay for it. The implicit assumption was that efficiency is the enemy of creative excellence, whereas in my view it is the other way round. I was Chairman of the Tate for 10 years and I would say that Nicholas Serota, the Director for that time, demonstrated that efficiency is the handmaiden and concomitant of artistic excellence.

There is often a presumption that in the 'blue corner' is something called creativity which is unstructured, untrammelled, free-flowing and loose, and in the 'red corner' is something that is boring, bureaucratic and efficient. Yet the most exciting organisations are those that are efficient and creative.

My 20s and 30s were spent building businesses. I started my first business when I was 25 and for the next ten years was involved in another fifteen or so start-ups. So I was a starter of businesses and then for some reason or other, as I got older, I got involved in corporate business. I'm now Chairman of three large businesses.

Another assumption people make is that small entrepreneurial businesses are creative and big businesses are bureaucratic and therefore uncreative. There is perhaps some justification for that mindset, because once you set up an organisation and need to have controls and standards of behaviour, you do run the risk of dumbing down and discouraging people from taking risks. But I would not accept that it is a necessary antithesis.

Bravery is very important in big companies. I think it was a brave and perhaps creative act to make Marjorie Scardino Chief Executive of Pearson – not least because her own hallmarks are bravery and creativity. She wasn't even in the running at first. Then after she was appointed the analysts wrote rude reports, the share price went down and we had to convene a hasty meeting of the analysts. But it was perfectly obvious she was the right person and incidentally a very brave and creative person. We didn't realise that she would be the first woman to run a FTSE company. We just chose an outstanding person for the job.

Let's switch to the Halifax which is a mature business in a mature industry, but which I would say I believe is also behaving in a brave and creative way. Our strategy is to treat consolidation – mergers and acquisitions – as guilty until proved innocent. We think it has destroyed value on both sides of the Atlantic and the opportunity cost is huge at a time when we ought to be changing our business strategy. This is so obvious it hardly bears saying. Yet because pressures towards aggregation are so strong, it is the only real game most other banks are playing. So we are definitely swimming against the conventional tide.

Secondly, we are saying that this is an industry which has been badly, or at best averagely, managed all over the world. So another part of our strategy is to transform the quality of the management in this business and thereby transform the performance. The first sign of that was to hire Andy Hornby, at the tender age of 33, to run all of what most people know as the Halifax. Was that creative? It was certainly brave because putting someone in charge of 20,000 people whose average age is several years older than his, is not the most obvious thing to do.

And the third part of the strategy is to become a venture capitalist in our own industry, which means seeing the new technology as an opportunity not a threat. It is about being brave enough to take advantage of the opportunity that has been given to us to put our money and our expertise into a new area, and so increase our market share. So we have invested £2 billion, not in new divisions but in totally new ventures.

The Halifax strategy is radical, it's bold and it breaks the mould, and if creativity means doing things differently, I suppose it is creative. Creativity is also partly about having the courage to do what other people might not see as obvious.

Many people think creativity is about lateral thinking – the 'off the wall, left of field' idea. There is a place for thinking the unthinkable but it is quite a small place.

I was involved in building two new towns in the North of England many years ago. My new towns were of course wonderful but the new town I most admired was Milton Keynes. The Milton Keynes New Town Corporation was a fantastic place, run by people who were constantly breaking the conventional rules. The reason Milton Keynes is now so big is that when they designed it they did it in four quadrants and they persuaded the government to allow them to start all four quadrants at the same time so it could never be reined in. Then the oil crisis hit and they had built this enormous place which depended on the car. They had a very bright young American called Lee Shostack who, as it was explained to me by his Chairman, Jock Campbell, had a very clever idea. They put a petrol station in each of the four quadrants, on what would turn out to be very important strategic sites for the petrol companies, and offered to give the land away as long as the petrol companies sold petrol at a large discount for a period of time. So everyone goes into Milton Keynes to get their petrol and the shopping centre is saved and Milton Keynes is saved. Once a clever person has seen the obvious under your nose, it seems even more obvious. Lee Shostack had a lateral mind and there is undoubtedly a place for that.

Some might say that my attitude to Chairmanship is creative. I believe that if you are a part-time Chairman you should not have an office or any infrastructure. You either get on so well with the Chief Executive that you perch on their desk and you trust their secretary to open all your post, or one of you has to go. I have a deal with the Chief Executive, which is very simple: you take all the decisions and I will back you through thick and thin, even when I do not agree with them. The quid pro quo is that I have to feel so involved in the thinking behind the decisions that I have my chance to influence any decision taken. And the final part of the contract is that I reserve the right to fire you; however if I do shoot you, I'll shoot you from the front and you'll be the first to hear! I stood up and told the 1,500 top managers of the Halifax at the Birmingham Conference Centre about my contract with James Crosby, the Chief Executive. They all seemed to love it and they could tell it was the truth. They felt good about having a Chairman and Chief Executive with that kind of relationship. I think that may be creative because it's redefining the roles of Chairman and Chief Executive. There is nothing lateral about it, however. It is about going back to first principles and thinking clearly about the realities of the relationship so as to avoid the obvious pitfalls.

I am a believer in thinking things through from first principles, without preconceptions if you are to achieve the best results. The 45-minute essay in British university exams where you are forced to be profoundly logical and argue from first principles still has a lot going for it. It's about bringing to bear clear thinking without woolliness and self-indulgence. Having sorted out the thinking, a second 'must' is to set about your business in such a way that you involve whoever you think the key constituency is – those who have to believe in it to do it. These constituencies can also stimulate, improve and add to what you have dreamed up. And, of course, there is no substitute for having a leadership or decision-making system that is prepared to be brave.

One of the reasons this does not often happen in large-scale business is the problem of large-scale business and the stock market. The UK and US stock markets are often dysfunctional. When our children and grandchildren write economic social history, they will be savage about the current imperative for financial engineering in public companies and they will say that we allowed ourselves to be controlled by a collection of vested interests. This is a personal view but I believe it strongly.

When somebody takes over as Chief Executive of some great company, they ought to be in a position to think through from first principles – what is it that the company is trying to produce, for whom and how? They have a responsibility to try and get it right which in no way conflicts with making money for themselves. However, with some honourable exceptions the people running large corporations on both sides of the Atlantic are short term and opportunistic in their thinking. The American Express platinum card culture that has gripped western capitalism in a world of financial engineering, headhunters and short-term career moves, simply doesn't encourage a way of doing things differently or from first principles.

One of the reasons that high intelligence and high principles are rare in large-scale business is because it has not been attractive to be involved in corporate Britain or corporate America. The sort of people who govern a large corporation are often people who have found security in being part of something big and who have become adept at climbing higher and higher on the greasy pole. Ambition, justified by the end results (whatever the process), plus personal insecurity has prevented them from setting up their own business or from going off to do something that's not for profit, or changing their lifestyle.

We live in a country which has the most concentrated economy in the free world, where the system is incentivised by something called short term shareholder value. This has got very little to do with long term, or even medium term, shareholder value and it's got everything to do with getting out a share of the value before the music stops. It has little to do with the real creation of wealth.

Large corporations, on both sides of the Atlantic, have failed to create organic growth. Few businesses have managed to create their great empires by developing products and services that people really want and will pay above average margins for, and then reinvesting in more products and services. If you look at the *Fortune 500* companies, their wealth creation is often abysmal. Yet these great mergers and acquisitions go on day after day egged on by the investment banks.

Big companies will need to address organic growth and they will need to start exploring creative ways of incentivising the people working for them, via new compensation packages and new working practices, to build real wealth. The emphasis will be on creating an environment and an atmosphere where employees can feel good about working for big companies because people are more likely to be 'creative', in the sense of doing things differently, and brave when they feel good about where they're working. We need to be creative to get back into the wealth creation business.

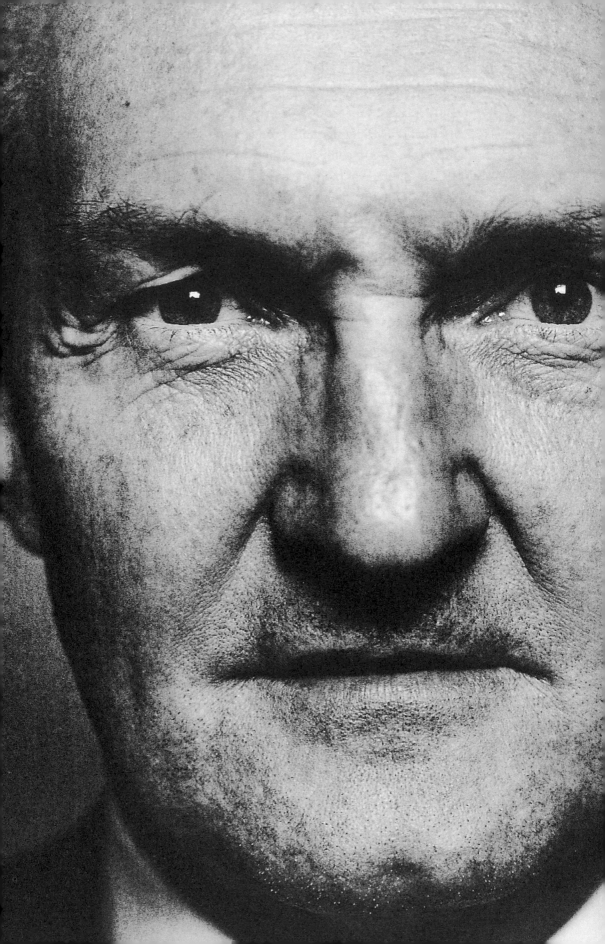

*J*ohn Sunderland is Chief Executive of Cadbury Schweppes plc. Cadbury Schweppes is a global confectionery and beverages company with a 1999 turnover of over £4 billion, pre-tax profits of nearly £700 million and 37,000 employees.

During his career with the company, he has worked extensively in both the confectionery and soft drinks sides of the business. He has served on the boards of Cadbury Ireland, Cadbury Schweppes South Africa, was a founding director of the Coca-Cola Schweppes joint venture in Great Britain, and was Managing Director of Trebor Bassett, created from the acquisition of a number of UK sugar confectionery companies.

In 1993 he became Managing Director of the Confectionery Stream and a member of the Cadbury Schweppes board. In September 1996 he was appointed to his current position.

John Sunderland

F or me creativity is the application of intelligence and imagination to problem solving. So the concept of there being a specific locus of creativity in a large corporation is nonsense. How can one discipline or function have a prerogative on that? Every function in business needs to be creative, whether it is in devising a new product or developing a new channel of distribution or improving the production line. Within business, creative adaptable thinking and problem solving is, in my view, a requirement of general management.

There might be more pockets of creativity in large corporations because size equals specialisation. Specialisation inevitably accrues to it skill sets, whereas in a smaller company people have to apply themselves more broadly across a far wider range of disciplines. A creative person in a small business will be applying his/her creativity across a panoply of different responsibilities. Look at a business like Pret à Manger and the degree of creativity that went into the concept, the product, the consumer relationships and the staff relationships – these were all new ways of doing things. So smallness can equal newness and newness implies creativity. In the creative services, such as advertising, there may be more functions which call upon creativity to a greater degree because they are creative solution providers to problems which are brought to them.

There's a big difference between an entrepreneur and a professional manager. We are hired hands at the end of the day, with an expertise which is broadly called management. An entrepreneur is a very different sort of animal and they don't join organisations like ours, or, if they do, they don't stay very long. We attract people who recognise that they're probably not entrepreneurs but are interested in the whole process of managing business and people. So they become professional managers of the creative process. It's about getting the best out of the human assets you have relative to whatever it is you're in business to do.

I don't think an organisation necessarily has to lose its

creativity as it gets bigger. Cisco is the largest company in the world at present and they are highly creative by my definition. They have completely rethought their whole way of doing business, from outsourcing the manufacturing process to new means of procurement. They challenged the status quo.

Ensuring you have people with the ability to challenge the status quo requires a brand of creativity that can be quite hard to engender in large businesses, but it's critical. You need to encourage innovative thinking throughout the organisation, because in the end no one person can carry the mandate for being creative. You need to programme iconoclasm into your organisation.

There is no reason why you can't try to make creative thinking part of your business process. Strategic development processes start with data analysis to understand what exactly is going on in the market, how competitively advantaged you are within it and what the emerging issues are. That can then act as a springboard for creative thinking by requiring people to think in alternative ways and exploring different strategic options for going forward.

There is a whole new alternative world that's springing up all around us. Harvard graduates don't want to join McKinsey, let alone Procter & Gamble, any more; they want to join that new breed of entrepreneurs who identify new creative opportunities. Large companies can try to accommodate this. We're trying to do this within Cadbury Schweppes through the availability of what we call a 'seed corn fund'. This makes substantial funding available for anybody that has a relevant new business idea. In a sense we're acting like venture capitalists capitalising our own people as a way of encouraging them. We have a very bright guy who we've just set up in business acting as an internal agent for all of our companies worldwide, for products which the principal company in the market doesn't want to sell. He's doing very well because he is a free agent.

When an idea carries with it the authority of the Chief Executive it can make people think and encourage the process by example.

Niall Fitzgerald is experimenting with Unilever in ways which are quite interesting. It was imaginative to offer the end product as a service through myhome.co.uk. There is considerable creativity in anticipating change and the timing of when you make your move. That is very critical with new technology because people often get ahead of the game. I'm sure myhome.co.uk is a valid concept – time poor, cash rich – but will it work today? I don't know and it doesn't matter; what's important is that you try these things.

People are experimenting with the problem of size in a fragmenting world. We're challenging ourselves in the way we do business and the way we employ people. I don't hold out Cadbury Schweppes as a role model for this, but it's certainly one of the issues that we recognise.

I've always maintained that one of the greatest dangers of size or time duration is custom and practice. Whenever anybody joins us, or goes to a new job, I always say they've got six months before they go native. I tell them to write down all of their first impressions, the opportunities, the way things are done, and keep referring to them, because in six months they'll be subsumed within the organisation's custom and practice. Once you've gone native it is hard to step out of the box again.

There are organisations which accept that's the way things are and they just carry on in a rather monolithic and congealed way. Personally I feel leadership is about trying to get the organisation to resist those sorts of forces. Having said that creating an environment where challenge is encouraged is easier said than done. People don't like to change or be taken out of their comfort zone.

But what never ceases to amaze me is how you can keep going back and challenging the status quo of the organisation and keep finding new and different ways to do things that really can take the organisation forward again.

Leadership is about going beyond management and inspiring a team of people to want to be better, to do more, to be more creative, to be the best. Creative leaders can be difficult people. People forget how Churchill was one of the most distrusted figures in 20th-century British politics, and yet an utterly inspired leader.

I think America is far ahead of the rest of the world in business and moving even further ahead with the new industrial revolution. In my view their biggest creative asset is their ability to reinvent themselves without any of the social hindrance that has been imposed upon cultures in the rest of the industrial world, particularly in parts of Europe and Japan, and, to a lesser extent, in Britain. American industry has down-sized around 70 million people over the last decade and re-absorbed all of them into new work. The rest of the industrial societies of the world have been unable to regenerate themselves like that because they carry too much social baggage about employment.

The face of business will change here because we now have a generation of children that are growing up knowing infinitely more than their parents about something which is truly important. They are growing up to be familiar with new technology and grasping its implications in an everyday way. It's an extension of that truism that only the kids can work the video. I believe it has extraordinary implications for business. Bright young people will have far more opportunities to think about creating their own business and not only will the opportunity for material gain be instilled in them but also the fact that you really can do it. So the future may well be more entrepreneurial. And business start-ups are undoubtedly a measure of commercial creativity.

The graduate employment hierarchy used to be investment banking, then the professions or consultancy and then blue chip businesses like ours. That's all changing now; there's a sense of 'go and do it for yourself'. It means that everyone has dropped down a division. There's new action out there and young people want to see it, feel it and try it.